T0362969

PUBLISHED BY BOOM BOOKS

boombooks.biz

ABOUT THIS SERIES

....But after that, I realised that I knew very little about these parents of mine. They had been born about the start of the Twentieth Century, and they died in 1970 and 1980. For their last 20 years, I was old enough to speak with a bit of sense.

I could have talked to them a lot about their lives. I could have found out about the times they lived in. But I did not. I know almost nothing about them really. Their courtship? Working in the pits? The Lock-out in the Depression? Losing their second child? Being dusted as a miner? The shootings at Rothbury? My uncles killed in the War? Love on the dole? There were hundreds, thousands of questions that I would now like to ask them. But, alas, I can't. It's too late.

Thus, prompted by my guilt, I resolved to write these books. They describe happenings that affected people, real people. The whole series is, to coin a modern phrase, designed to push your buttons, to make you remember and wonder at things forgotten.

The books might just let nostalgia see the light of day, so that oldies and youngies will talk about the past and re-discover a heritage otherwise forgotten. Hopefully, they will spark discussions between generations, and foster the asking and answering of questions that should not remain unanswered.

BORN IN 1969?
WHAT ELSE HAPPENED?

RON WILLIAMS

AUSTRALIAN SOCIAL HISTORY

BOOK 31 IN A SERIES OF 35
FROM 1939 to 1973

War Babies Years (1939 to 1945): 7 Titles
Baby Boom Years (1946 to 1960): 15 Titles
Post Boom Years (1961 to 1973): 13 Titles

BOOM, BOOM BABY, BOOM

Born in 1969? What else happened?

Published by Boom Books

Wickham, NSW, Australia

Web: www.boombooks.biz

© Ron Williams 2012. This printing 2023.

Creator: Williams, Ron, 1934- author

Title: Born in 1969? : what else happened? / Ron Williams.

Series: Born in series, book 31.

ISBN: 9780648324461

Australia--History--Society and social sciences--20th century.

Cover images: With thanks to the National Archives of Australia: A1200, L80289, Joe Bjelke-Petersen, Queensland Premier; A1200, L79657, tennis champion Margaret Court; A1501, A10014, Australian Army jungle training; A1200, L59470, author Ruth Park.

TABLE OF CONTENTS

IMPORTANT PEOPLE AND EVENTS

Queen of England	Elizabeth II
Prime Minister of Australia	John Gorton
Leader of Opposition	Gough Whitlam
Governor General	Sir Paul Hasluck
Pope	Paul VI
PM of England	Harold Wilson
President of America	Richard Nixon
Emperor of Japan	Hirohito

WINNER OF THE ASHES

1968	Drawn	1 - 1
1970 -71	England	2 - 0
1972	Drawn	2 - 2

MELBOURNE CUP WINNERS

1968	Rainlover
1969	Rainlover
1970	Baghdad Note

ACADEMY AWARDS

Best Actor	Cliff Robertson
Best Actress	Katherine Hepburn

PREFACE TO THIS SERIES

This book is the 31st in a series of books that I have researched and written. It tells a story about a number of important or newsworthy Australia-centric events that happened in 1969. The series covers each of the years from 1939 to 1973 for a total of 35 books.

I developed my interest in writing these books a few years ago at a time when my children entered their teens. My own teens started in 1947, and I tried to remember what had happened to me then. I thought of the big events first, like Saturday afternoon at the pictures, and cricket in the back yard, and the wonderful fun of going to Maitland on the train for school each day.

Then I recalled some of the not-so-good things. I was an altar boy, and that meant three or four Masses a week. I might have thought I loved God at that stage, but I really hated his Masses. And the schoolboy bullies, like Greg Favel and the hapless Freddie Bevin. Yet, to compensate for these, there was always the beautiful, black headed, blue-sailor-suited June Brown, who I was allowed to worship from a distance.

I also thought about my parents. Most of the major events that I lived through came to mind readily. But after that, I realised that I really knew very little about these parents of mine. They had been born about the start of the Twentieth Century, and they died in 1970 and 1980. For their last 20 years, I was old enough to speak with a bit of sense. I could have talked to them a lot about their lives. I could have found out about the times they lived in. But I did not. I know almost nothing about them really. Their courtship? Working in the pits? The Lock-out in the Depression? Losing their second child? Being dusted as a miner? The shootings at Rothbury? My uncles killed in the War? There were hundreds, thousands of questions that I would now like to ask them. But, alas, I can't. It's too late.

Thus, prompted by my guilt, I resolved to write these books. They describe happenings that affected people, real people. In 1969, there is some coverage of international affairs, but a lot more on social events within Australia. This book, and the whole series is, to coin a modern phrase, designed to push the reader's buttons, to make you remember and wonder at things forgotten. The books might just let nostalgia see the light of day, so that oldies and youngies will talk about the past and re-discover a heritage otherwise forgotten. Hopefully, they will spark discussions between generations, and foster the asking and the answering of questions that should not remain unanswered.

The sources of my material. I was born in 1934, so that I can remember well a great deal of what went on around me from 1939 onwards. But of course, the bulk of this book's material came from research. That meant that I spent many hours in front of a computer reading electronic versions of newspapers, magazines, Hansard, Ministers' Press releases and the like. My task was to sift out, day-by-day, those stories and events that would be of interest to the most readers. Then I supplemented these with materials from books, broadcasts, memoirs, biographies, government reports and statistics. And I talked to old-timers, one-on-one, and in organised groups, and to Baby Boomers about their recollections. People with stories to tell came out of the woodwork, and talked no end about the tragic, and funny, and commonplace events that have shaped their families and lives.

The presentation of each book. For each year covered, the end result is a collection of short Chapters on many of the topics that concerned ordinary people in that year.

I think I have covered most of the major issues that people then were interested in. On the other hand, in some cases I have dwelt a little on minor frivolous matters, perhaps to the detriment of more sober considerations. Still, in the long run, this makes the book more readable, and hopefully it will convey adequately the spirit of the times.

Each of the books is mainly Sydney based, but I have been **deliberately national in outlook**, so that readers elsewhere will feel comfortable that I am talking about matters that affected them personally. After all, housing shortages and strikes and juvenile delinquency involved **all** Australians, and other issues, such as problems overseas, had no State component in them. I expect I can make you wonder, remember, rage and giggle equally, no matter whence you hail.

INTRODUCTION TO 1969

A few carry-over situations from 1968 are worthy of mention. The main story of 1968, and for a couple of years before that, was the war in Vietnam. On paper, this looked like a civil war where the North and the South were having a dust-up to see who would get control of the nation. I suppose there is some element of truth in that, but it is not the whole truth or anything like it.

Really, it was the battle **between Communism** on the one hand **and Capitalism** on the other. The Reds, clearly the Baddies from the viewpoint of Australia and America, had **armies** from China and North Vietnam, as well as **guerillas** from the North. The Goodies had armed forces from South Vietnam, backed up by fighters and armaments from the USA, Australia, and a dozen half-hearted nations.

For the two Vietnamese nations, the fight was about **getting rid of the Dutch who had controlled them for two or more centuries**. All over the world, the locals were trying to get rid of their former colonial masters, and often this wish for freedom was mixed in with Communist insurgence so that no militant was quite sure whether he was fighting for Communism or for Nationalism.

For the other combatants, this was purely an ideological fight over which economic and political system was good for the world. The Communists (led by China) wanted a world that would be painted Red, while the Capitalists (led by America) wanted to see free enterprise and opportunism rule across the Seven Seas.

For these latter countries, Vietnam was the ideal place to somehow prove that their own system of choice was the better. And, of course, **the best way to do this was to fight a vicious war on someone else's territory**. Vietnam was the lucky nation that suited the purposes of both the Reds and the Yanks.

So, a few years ago, fighting between the parties started and increased now to massive proportions. Sometimes one side said it was winning, and sometimes the other claimed to be on top. **By now, no one was very interested in the military side of it.**

But, from the viewpoint of the Goodies, every nation that was fighting had about **half its population who supported the war, and half who opposed it**. Australia was torn down the middle, as was the USA. Britain, for once, did not send troops, and this annoyed the USA. But even in Britain, there were big numbers who wanted to join the fight and stop the nasty Reds from ruling the world.

In Australia, **the opposition to the war** came from people who could see no reason for it. And, importantly, it came **from families of all the young men who had been drafted to fight it, and perhaps to die, for whatever reason**. **The supporters** wanted to see Communism dealt a major blow, and thought that if the Reds won up there, then they would sweep down through the south-west Pacific, and collect Australia on the way.

The effect in Australia was that, **for once**, this nation was galvanised into political activity. Everyone had a choice. **Either you were for or against the war.** If you spoke or wrote in favour of one side or the other, you were immediately attacked by anyone within reach. Supporters on either side were marching and demonstrating almost daily, and many of these events ended in scuffles and punch-ups. The Letters to the Newspapers were full of arguments, some of them sensible, and most of them full of emotional dross.

In short, the war in Vietnam, at the start of 1969, was the major focus for the entire nation, and would continue to be just that for the rest of the year. As we proceed though this book, we will watch with interest as all sorts of developments spring to life.

THE PILL IN 1969

By now, the Pill had been around for a few years, and had gained acceptance among many women. A lot of these, who wanted it for family planning purposes, were satisfied with its workings, and those who wanted it for a freer sex life were also satisfied, provided they remembered to take it all the time.

There were a few problems reported when small children helped themselves to supplies and were rushed dramatically to hospital. And other reported cases of young girls getting their pills mixed up, and taking the wrong ones for a time. There was also a young girl who claimed that, despite her taking the Pill as required, she had got pregnant and was currently suing her doctor and the manufacturer. All in all, though, its launch here had been quite successful.

There were, however, some women who stayed away. Many of these were Catholics. About half of these did this because they were convinced that there were **elements in their faith that forbade its use**.

Others did it **only because** the Catholic Church banned its use. They were not convinced by any argument the Church put forward. They accepted the ban only because the Church, with all of its authority, told them too. These women were torn between their natural instincts on the one hand, and the restraints of the Church on the other. Many of them accepted the Pill after much mental anguish. This in turn led some to have a different attitude to their Church, and quite a few stopped practising as a consequence.

OUR 1968 PRIME MINISTER

The current Prime Minister was John Gorton. He had been elected by his fellow Parliamentarians, and in his lethargic style, was holding the fort quite well. He only held that position for three years, in a period when the Opposition Party, Labor, was just starting to pull itself together after twenty years in the wilderness.

The up and coming Leader of the Labor Party, responsible for its re-birth, was the young Gough Whitlam, who some of you might have heard of.

PROSPECTS FOR SPACE TRAVEL

Over the previous decade, both the Russians and the Americans **had made great steps forward in moving into space**. One or other of them each year had some announcement that it had done something spectacular. Satellites had been fired into space, and gone around the earth, and had come back safe. They had done the same thing with men aboard. A dog planned to do the same thing, and got up into orbit, but has never been seen again. Satellites had gone around the moon, and photographed the dark side. **It had been all go-go for the Sixties.**

But now, **there were reports that America would be sending men to the moon**. That mankind would actually **land on the moon**. America's space agency, NASA, will have a lot of egg on its face if it does not do something soon.

SEWAGE STILL A PROBLEM

At the end of 1968, the nation had a sewage problem that was ever so slowly being addressed.

Letters, L Schultz. If we don't admit there is Harbour pollution, it is not likely to be stopped. On Wednesday, it was reported that Mr Gay, the town clerk of Mosman, had said that "tests taken each month in five tidal pools in the municipality had always been favourable."

I don't know what Mr Gay means by favourable, but if he comes to Clifton Gardens pool, when wind and tide conditions are suitable, he won't need to do any tests: he will see sewage floating in the baths. Maybe the effluent has a favourable bacteriological count, but few people like swimming among sewage matter, whatever the bacteriological count may be.

Comment. Of course the authorities were aware of this, and of course they would have liked to fix it. But we had so many aspects of our lives where long distances and huge areas needed our attention and development, and we had such a small population to bear the financial burden.

I am afraid that if you are not in a city, you will have to wait a while, say 20 years, before the dunny out the back gives way to an indoor toilet.

BREATH TESTS

The testing of breath for motorists involved in accidents was just coming to the various States. They were in the process of introducing legislation and regulations that imposed penalties if a driver had a test result of over .10 per cent, and imposing various penalties on him.

There was considerable debate on this move imposed by authorities, and most motorists had not yet come to accept it. Still, some did.

> Letters, C McKellar. A leading article in the British Medical Journal of October 26, 1968, comments on the fall of mortality to be seen on the roads in Britain. It notes a satisfactory fall in mortality is to be seen on the roads. The Chief Medical Officer notes 'a striking reduction' in the last quarter of 1967 after the introduction of alcohol tests.
>
> But, as for other killers, outstanding among these is still tobacco, the main cause of lung cancer. The death rate from this disease again rose among both men and women in 1967... all told some 28,000 persons died of it in the year under review."

Comment. I think that most people now fully accept drink-driving legislation as a good thing.

The above Letter also points out the link between smoking on the one hand and lung cancer and other illnesses on the other. This was also a battle in its early stages. Much water would flow under the bridge before most people would be convinced, and indeed there would still be some today who reject or ignore the link.

MY RULES IN WRITING

Now we are just about ready to go. First, though, I give you a few Rules I follow as I write. They will help you understand where I am coming from.

Note. Throughout this book, I rely a lot on reproducing **Letters from the newspapers**. Whenever I do this, I put the text in a different font, and indent it a little, and make the font somewhat smaller. **I do not edit the text at all. The same is true for the** News Items **at the start of each Chapter.** That is, I do not correct spelling or if the text gets at all garbled, I do not correct it. It's just as it was seen in the Papers.

Second Note. The **material** for this book, when it comes from newspapers, is reported as it was seen at the time. If the benefit of hindsight over the years changes things, then I might record that in my Comments. **The info reported thus reflects matters as they were seen in 1969.**

Third Note. Let me also apologise in advance to anyone I might offend. In a work such as this, it is certain some people will think **I got some things wrong. I am sure that I did**, but please remember, all of this is only my opinion. And really, **my opinion does not matter one little bit in the scheme of things. I hope you will say "silly old bugger", and shrug your shoulders, and read on.**

OFF WE GO

So now we are ready to plunge into 1969. **Let's go**, and I trust you will have a pleasant trip.

JANUARY NEWS ITEMS

Citizens in the New Year awoke to the news that the Queen had appointed **15 new Knights and one Dame** in her Honours list. Names you might recognise were Cardinal **Norman Gilroy, Macfarlane Barnett, and John (Black Jack) McEwan. Sportsmen Heather McKay (squash) and Les Favell (cricket)** also received lesser Honours.

This good news was dampened by the **crash of a Viscount** airliner, landing at Port Hedland in Western Australia. **All 26 passengers and crew were killed**.

The NSW Government will introduce **a new scheme to reduce the road toll.** Motorists found guilty of road offences will be docked **a certain number of points.** When their total points docked in a given time reaches a limit, their licence will be removed for a period....

It is not **certain** that the scheme will be introduced as yet. A spokesman added that **three radar speed testing machines** had arrived, and will be tested soon....

It is likely that persons found guilty, of speeding, using the radar equipment, will lose points if the new points-scheme is introduced. **Isn't science grand....**

He went on to reassure the public that these measures were to reduce the road toll, and **not for revenue raising.**

Police say they have discovered **the body of a fourth baby in bushland areas** near the NSW small country city of Gosford. **Three other young bodies have been found in the last month....**

Police are **also searching for the bodies of two other young children in the locality.** It is believed that a mother **gave birth to six children over the last seven years**, and that she had disposed of their bodies over that period. **Investigations are proceeding.**

America suffered its first plane hijacking of the year on January 4th. A routine ex-Washington passenger flight was diverted to Miami. 138 passengers were involved. The gunman was held at the Havana airport. **Last year in America, there were 18 hijackings....**

Meanwhile, another flight was diverted from Athens to Cairo after **a shot was fired through the window of the pilot's cabin.** Again the gunman was held by police....

There was a rash of hijackings at the time. All villains thought that somehow they could bargain their way to something better. None of them ever did.

At the Warragamba African Lion Park Safari, near Sydney, **a lion cub was born to a sick mother.** She was too ill to feed it. Feeding it with **an eye dropper** was not working. The cub was put in with a **feeding mother cat**, but after a day, it had to be removed because it was not getting enough milk....

It was then put in with **a nursing mother corgi**, who gave it preference over her own litter. But to little avail, and **the cub died on the next day. The mother corgi whined for a few hours**, but returned in full to her own litter next day.

GROUP THINK AIN'T ALL BAD

Before I go on to the delights of the NSW countryside, let me point out that right now is the very peak of the Great Australian Summer Break. That means that almost everyone has packed up and gone somewhere else for a few weeks on holiday.

One consequence of this is that the newspapers relax a bit so that their normal incessant messages of doom and despair give way to talk about knitting patterns and recipes.

Thus there are no sensations coming from the Press, and that leaves me, for this month only, to **ramble on about anything I like. I indulge myself.**

That is exactly what I am going to do for a few pages.

But I should warn you first, that I really mean **ramble**. I have no message I want to give you, and no idea at all about saving the world.

If, tomorrow, I find that I have written rubbish, I will delete the few pages. **So, if you find four blank pages here on the morrow, you know what happened.**

So, off to Bong Bong and whatever flows from that.

Bong Bong is about 300 kms south west of Sydney. 150 years ago there was a small township there, but as the road and rail routes between Sydney and Melbourne changed, it gradually faded away, and the only visible sign of it now is a Church used for services for tourists.

Why mention it? Back in 1969, and for many years after, one of the great events of Sydney social scene was the Bong Bong Picnic Races. This annual spectacle attracted the smart Sydney middle class down the Hume Highway for a day of drinking and gambling at a nearby race track that was resurrected especially for the race-day. Office workers by their thousands grabbed their wicker baskets full of grog, told their management that they had the flu, and headed south west to Bong Bong. Where, by chance, a number of horses went round the track a few times, but that never spoilt the joyous occasion.

All this is mildly interesting, but so what? In 1969, Bong Bong became the centre of a controversy that had repercussions well beyond the race track. It concerned the usage of speedboats on the nearby small body of water known as the Bong Bong Reservoir. Various Authorities involved with Lands, and with Wildlife and Animal Welfare ,had influenced the local Council to ban the boats.

In doing this, the Council had accepted arguments relating to noise, and the amount of wash and therefore erosion, and the damage to wildlife, especially platypuses and bird-life. **Not all Councillors agreed.** One of the dissidents argued that only one mile of riverbank was affected by wash. Another argued that the most of the time the river and dam were stagnant and that the boats stirred up the river and made it healthier.

Another Letter writer pointed out that boating on Bong Bong provided good opportunities for youth to engage in a healthy sport. But another person said that 15 miles away there was a very big lake, much better suited to motor boats, and not prone to the supposed problems at Bong Bong.

To a reader 50 years later, all of these arguments are fully familiar. They are hardly worthy of reporting in the media.

That was not the case then. Let me develop this thought.

Letters, P Edwards. The controversies flare up and die down, the arguments vary: Colong Caves or limestone, Myall Lakes national park or rutile mining, wildlife or water ski-ing at Bong Bong. These are not isolated incidents, but manifestations of an enormous problem facing humanity.

The problem is to adapt our thinking to the changed nature of the human occupation of the earth. **Once**, exploitation was localised, the scars healed, and the prodigality of nature could be depended on to provide future needs. **Now,** it is nature which is localised -- fragments so far unnoticed by the exploiters, bits of national park, pieces of reserve. We must realise that the pressure of human population on remaining resources is such that old priorities have changed. **The most precious things we now possess are fresh air, clean water and the irreplaceable resources of scenery and living things.**

It is ironical that science, which has given man the tools to rapidly destroy his environment, has also, by an expected flight to the moon, given him a clearer concept of the uniqueness and value of the earth as man's home.

This is the good earth which conservationists are fighting to save for future humanity.

Here is an early first local rumbling of environmentalism **as an organised movement**. Prior to this, there had been complaints against **the destruction or co-option** of the worlds around us as if there was no future to come. Examples abound of roads cutting through forests, of bowling clubs capturing public space, of new industries building on open areas, of forests being cleared for coalmines, of housing developments ousting and destroying communities. The list could go on and on.

But at the end of the Sixties, as exemplified by Bong Bong and Mr Edwards' Letter, our worthy citizens collectively were waking up to the need for more public discussion of environmental issues, and the need for greater control over all sorts of development. Up until the late Sixties, any one with a gripe about developments, launched a solitary battle against it. Lots of **individuals fought battles** over the years against lots of projects.

Now, however, such individuals were realising that the power of **combining with others of similar mind** to put pressure on decision makers **might** sometimes work. Individuals were joining small groups, small groups were liaising with larger groups, and larger groups were recruiting individuals. Not through political parties, but **through the unity of a cause**.

It was a time when **attitudes were fast changing right across the nation.** This normally easy-going nation was being split into two by the Vietnam crisis, and normally relaxed and **devil-may-care attitudes were giving way to serious thought**. The realisation was dawning that if things were wrong, there was no hope that one person alone could make changes. Instead united action, taken in conjunction with strangers, could make a difference.

So, pleas like that of Mr Edwards were being listened to. For example, women who felt they should have a better deal, were becoming active to get it. **Individual** authors, patron saints like Betty Friedan and Germaine Greer, were nevertheless giving way to women's **movements, feminists were being replaced by Feminists**. The same was true for **the environment and animal welfare**.

Nowhere was this more obvious than in the way Aborigines took a great step forward in gaining a measure of social justice in the late Sixties. Governments, State and Federal, legislated and manipulated to make significant changes and this was the result of long campaigns **orchestrated** by **organised bodies**.

So, I come to the point that I am making. In the late 1960's, *Pressure Groups* **were replacing pushy** *individuals. Complaints* **were being converted into** *causes.* **Arguments were no longer** *about right and wrong***, they were now about** *political power*.

It was the beginning of a social metamorphosis that has carried through, with increasing momentum, to this very day. **Bong Bong reasoning has gone.** Instead, social groups, and pressure groups, and party politics, dominate our news and thinking and what our world will look like.

Comment from tomorrow. Maybe this **is** all a bit too serious for the holiday period. **But I will not delete it.** So there are no blank pages. But I do promise, for a while, I will lighten up a bit.

HEART TRANSPLANTS

Over the last few years a number of surgeons, and their teams of experts, had conducted heart transplants in specialist hospitals across the world. Some of these were successful, and some were not.

These operations were right at the forefront of medical technology and represented major break-throughs. Not surprisingly, there were different opinions on the ethics of this. I will let you sort out the arguments from the Letters below.

Letters, Kempson Maddox. Very few experienced physicians would be prepared confidently to predict when heart failure is irreversible and before agreeing to a heart transplant would wish to know the duration and quality of life after the operation.

The longer Australian surgeons can be persuaded **to refrain** from attempts at cardiac transplantation, and Australian patients from accepting them, the **better chance there will be** that more experienced centres overseas will reveal the true value of these experiments, and the measure of control of the inevitable hazards which follow them.

At present, the extreme cost in manpower and hospital care **would be better devoted to prevention of heart disease** in the manner advocated by the National Heart Foundation.

Letters, Harry Windsor. Sir Kempson suggests that Australian activities in the matter of heart transplantation be confined to an appraisal of work done in large overseas centres. I would remind Sir

Kempson in appraising the results in the first 25 people who had transplants in the great centres, 18 lived a shorter time and 14 lived less than one week.

In cardiac surgery one has always to answer the question as to what a patient will be like after operation. The answer is always a hopeful one. However in the matter of transplantation, I can assure Sir Kempson that the day is far in the future when assurance of a long and normal post-operative life can be given.

Sir Kempson is concerned that cost, manpower, and care would be better devoted to **prevention** of heart disease. Let Nobel Laureate, Sir Peter Medawar, reply. When asked about the cost of transplants when 99 per cent of world population cried out for elementary medical care, he said: "Great advances in medicine must nowadays start with great capital investment of time, money and energy. **The heroic adventures of today are part of tomorrow's ordinary medical care.**"

Letters, P Manzie. Another trend lies close to the heart of this dispute - the massive growth of medicine's administrative tail, fostered by bureaucratic disposal of money. The healing industry must surpass most others in **the proportion of personnel who are not where the action is**. More doctors become less keen to serve in the front line. Research carries the magic, captures brains; although some of its findings are esoteric, and most will do no more than add to the already vast store of undistributed techniques.

Thus, the brighter the medical student, the greater his chance of leading a useless life; while humanity cries out for elementary medical help.

At this moment of history, are not heart transplants a silly use of human cleverness? Under the walls of hospitals, in which these tours de force are enacted, live dozens who could benefit from diversion of a fraction of the cost. Dr Windsor's quote - "The heroic adventures of today are part of tomorrow's ordinary medical care" - has a strangely antique, Wellsian flavour. **Surely, man's problem, in this over-crowded planet, is to ensure that tomorrow does come.** Applied sciences are the ones that matter. Medical talents need to concentrate on the philosophy, and methods, of distribution.

Comment. The above coverage of a growing issue is not meant to be comprehensive or complete. Indeed, at this stage, it would scarcely be possible to do this. I offer the Letters only as examples of the embryonic thinking that had occurred so far.

However, looking at things 50 years later, it appears that transplantation has indeed triumphed. Thus there are operations to swap good parts for bad for all organs of the human body, for tens of thousands of people everywhere.

I can't guess what might have happened if the research money been put to other purposes, but I find it hard, even with benefit of hindsight, to suggest what those purposes might be.

Second Comment. One of the **philosophical problems** that transplantation gave rise to, was a religious one. For example, if parts of the body could be swapped round, **where does the soul lie?** If you swapped legs, the soul clearly lay with the whole. But is this true if you swapped hearts? **And what if you swapped brains?**

These questions seemed remote at this stage, but academics and theologians were starting to dwell on them. I hope you will excuse me if I don't.

VIETNAM ALREADY

The *SMH* published its first Vietnam Letters for the year on January 2nd, Then there was another slew on January 4th. In fact, Vietnam continued to be the most talked about issue, so that the Letters continued on all through the year.

I will not attempt to keep up with the Letters or the war-time news as they unfold. Every now and then, I will pick out some story or make some point, and so my coverage in the Book will not be a day by day chronicle. The fact, however, that I do not give this war much space should not be seen as suggesting the war was not important. It most certainly was, and I ask you to keep that at the back of your mind as a I twitter along about lesser matters.

I will get the ball rolling with just these two Letters to give you more background as to where the controversy lies.

Letters, Zofiz Zuzman. I am all for democratic privileges and, to prove it, I give them sometimes an airing **by way of protesting**, as I believe that freedoms when not used tend to get mouldy and eventually disintegrate.

I can't see, however, why I should call on Mum's son to go to far away places, get killed or, worse, be made a murderer of innocent people who have never done me or him any harm, in order to defend us. I am not a pacifist and would resist anybody who threatens my country's integrity and that's exactly what the Vietnamese are doing in their own land.

My patriotism is limited to defending Australia for the Australians, but not stretched enough to defend Vietnam against the Vietnamese.

Letters, Michael Boylan. A friend of mine is serving 29 days in Long Bay Gaol for refusing to attend a National Service medical examination. Another will soon be dismissed from the Public Service for failing to produce a National Service registration certificate. **Both face two years' gaol for their non-compliance with this Act.** Their crime is to believe that conscription for the Vietnam war is morally wrong, and if it is a crime **to believe**, then we are all in danger.

For their punishment is more than wasted days in gaol. It is a criminal record and the automatic exclusion from many jobs that this entails, it is a file in the office of ASIO, and the refusal of a security clearance. I know applicants for scholarships and certain positions who have been asked to explain their presence at various meetings, in various picket lines, and why they associate with certain people. Isn't this the denial of freedom of speech, of thought, of assembly?

This is what it is like, then, to live in a repressive

society: the fear that I feel for myself and for my friends.

ADVENTURES IN SPACE

It looks like the US is going to blast off toward the moon soon. The writer below asks the question that is puzzling many others.

Letters, Fred Aarons. The "Herald's" thought-provoking leader, "The good earth", concerning the lunar expedition of the US astronauts should cause many people to ponder not only their individual relationship with their environment, but that of the latter within the limitless expanse of the universe.

Our astonishment and admiration should not inhibit the question put in parallel circumstances by a Roman philosopher: For what good? (Cui bono?) - more especially as two noted scientists have, since the lunar flight, cast serious doubts upon the wisdom or usefulness of the great adventure. **Sir Bernard Lovell has said that a moon landing would add little to human knowledge; and the President of the American Association for the Advancement of Science thinks that the talent and money lavished on such adventures should be employed in human betterment.**

But "reason's comparing balance," introduced by Pope in his "Essay on Man," has no place in the field of international prestige; otherwise health, education and social development in general would take precedence over achievements in space, or, in Australia's case, over our futilities in Antartica.

CANDLES IN THE SKY

Letters, N McDonald. I was staggered to read - as thousands of other readers must have been - that the Commonwealth Bureau of Meteorology releases weather balloons carrying lighted candles over NSW bushland. This is a practice which can only be termed criminally insane, particularly when you remember that at least nine people have already died in NSW bushfires this summer and millions of dollars' worth of property destroyed.

Spokesmen for the bureau claim there is no danger of fire from these balloons because the candles are presumed to be extinguished before they reach the ground. Obviously the bureau has given no thought to a faulty balloon drifting slowly to earth. With its candle encased in highly inflammable waxed paper, it could very easily begin a fire.

Another grazier chimed in and said that the candles had started fires on his property in long **grass.** Though, he wrote, **it could be that lightning was really the cause**. He thought that lightening was most likely, but he considered the Weather Bureau as useless, so **he preferred to blame the candles**.

FEBRUARY NEWS ITEMS

Opponents of the new laws on drink-driving argue that **compulsory** blood tests should not be used because of British Law that **a person must not be forced to incriminate himself. Submitting to a blood test potentially does that.** It is the same law as the popular 5th Amendment loved by American TV movies....

That is one argument. **A different argument** is that the above is just one interpretation of British Law, and that **it does not apply here**. In any case, **it passed into all our Legislatures without much ado**.

An American man, described as an aerial photographer, **had been making counterfeit** US and Australian notes here for three years. He had uttered 300,000 Pounds of these. **He was to face Court for this today**....

Instead, he took a Single-engine Auster aircraft and **flew over Sydney for four hours.** He was in contact with the police all the while, and at times threatened suicide, to take sleeping pills, and to fly the plane out to sea till it crashed....

Police promised they would help him and he landed. **He was taken to Court, and sentenced to five years in a prison farm**, with psychiatric help.

In an attempt to reduce road deaths, the NSW Minister for Transport has now approved **the purchase of many new machines** that **can measure the speed that a car** is travelling when it passes a given point. In an extension of his earlier plans, he expects to **set up radar traps at many country locations.**

A Sydney skin-diver found the remnants **of a hull and two cannon on the bottom of Sydney Harbour**. They had been **there for 112 years**, and were identified as the remnants of an armed merchantman, called *Catherine Adamson,* lost in 1857 with the cost of 21 lives....

A day later **the cannon were confiscated** by the Commonwealth Government. The **Receiver of Wrecks** will hold them for a year and then **they will be auctioned**. **The diver will be allowed to bid for them.** The diver is reported to be "upset" at this news....

In future he **must report everything he takes, including nails**. Fines apply for each unreported item.

A sign of the times. An American soldier flew to Sydney to marry an Australian girl later that day. They will take a five-day honeymoon and he will then fly back to **the combat zone in Vietnam**. The pair met a year ago while he was on **R and R leave in Sydney**.

A news item from the **front-page** of the *SMH* said that **some nondescript person** in the **Russian** Public Service **had been dismissed because he was difficult to work** with. "Only in the most urgent cases will his fellow workers deal with him...."

I mention this here because it shows that **our Press**, along with the American Press, **were so desperate to spread anti-Communist propaganda**, that they made a completely trivial dismissal into front page news.

CONDITIONS IN PRISON

Letters, Elizabeth Donoghue. Are the Government and the community aware of the degrading conditions suffered by prisoners on remand in Sydney's metropolitan prisons?

These men are detained in custody because their families lack the means to pay the money required to secure their release while awaiting trial. A man in this position eats food no cheap restaurant would be permitted to serve. Fresh dairy produce or fruit is unknown. He can smoke only if his family or friends can afford to pay for his tobacco. He is not permitted such small necessities as toothpaste until he has been there for one month.

He is confined to his cell for 19 hours each day, given the freedom of a small yard for five. His cell measures three paces by four and is occupied by one or two other prisoners. Visitors may be received twice a week - during office hours, which automatically cancels one in many cases, and on Saturdays. The prisoner and his visitor cannot see and hear each other at the same time. They are separated by a glass partition, in which a strip of gauze, six inches high, is inserted, below eye level. Every word is overheard by the supervising officer or drowned out by the raised voices of other prisoners and their visitors. The visit is of 20 minutes.

And so a man awaits trial, suffering under conditions like those of a dog in a pound. Are these men presumed innocent until proven guilty?

Comment. This Letter stirred up only a few responses. Everyone agreed that conditions were tough, but most agreed that they were better than in the US and most of Asia and Europe.

But other writers **strayed** to another topic concerning those who had been found guilty, and were in prison. *Serves themselves right*, was the popular expressed attitude. If they had committed a crime, did they expect luxury? Jails were made as places of punishment and to discourage others from committing crimes.

It was not for decades that it was suggested that **such places could be used for rehabilitation that included training.**

And now, in 2019, the question remains unresolved. **Correction or punishment and revenge?** Can they be both? No point in asking me. It's an old argument that keeps on popping up with different faces. I have a foot in many camps, and my answer varies as I look at various individuals and the crimes they committed.

Perhaps **that** is the answer. Not to put prisoners into various categories, but to decide on an individual basis. In that case, someone needs **to tell me just who will be wise enough to do that. Judges? Prison Departments? Psychologists? Ministers of Justice? Clergy?**

I don't care much who you pick to do the job. Just not me.

WHO'S COUNTING

For twenty years, some people had been worrying about atomic bombs destroying the world. Lots of politicians have wanted do **something** to reduce the risk, lots of scientists had made names for themselves by talking about the science and the effects of bombs. Incessantly, newspapers sold billions of copies by scaring the populations of all nations with their fanciful tales about bombs and their aftermath.

That is one side of the story. But there is another side. This says that, with so many bombs being stock-piled by so many different countries, there is bound to be some nutter who lets a few atom bombs loose, and the retaliation will set the world on fire.

The differences between the two sides were vast. It does not matter here which side you think is right, what you should notice is **how far apart they were in the bomb count**, and you can believe me that this was true for all sorts of counts.

Letters, D Posener. The destructive capability of existing nuclear weapon stockpiles is very large indeed, but not as great as imagined by most people. Gross exaggeration by an apparently impeccable authority (L B Johnson, "My Years of Power,") is all the more startling in its implications.

The article quoted contends that the USA has available "the equivalent of about 30,000 tons of TNT **for every human being alive**." A more reasonable figure is 30 tons, which itself is impressive enough. The quoted value, applied to a world population of about 3,400 million, implies a total capability of about 100 million million tons TNT-equivalent; if only one per cent of all this were in the form of strategic missile warheads of one million tons TNT equivalent (and this is roughly the power of the predominant US weapons), it would follow that the USA is supposed to have about 1,000,000 such weapons.

Besides being about a thousand times more than the number generally accepted ("Time," November 8, 1968), this is simply beyond the bounds of credibility (if only because the cost, at about $10 million each, comes to some ten times the gross national product of the USA).

Comment. By 2018, the "don't worry" camp has won out so far. Since 1949, the count of bombs has gone up, and then in the last decade, down a bit. Still, there are enough devices to go round, so if anyone wants to set one off, probably few of us will be here to worry about it.

BREATH TEST LEGISLATION

Australia was **a young nation** among the countries of the Western World. When WWII came, we had been a nation for less than 40 years, and had formerly been a collection of colonies that were filled literally with wild colonial boys. No one could accuse us of being sophisticated, and much of the culture of Western Europe was still a long way from our shores.

After WWII, our military came home with chips firmly on their shoulders, and in fact, more resistant to authority than before the War. Their stories abounded with tales of how they had outwitted and mocked their stuck-up Pommy officers, and had broken all the norms expected in the British Army.

Twenty-odd years later, they were a fair bit wiser. **For example**, many had gotten themselves a much better education than their parents had dreamed of. The Federal Government had helped in this by providing free university places for many of the returning Diggers. On top of that, the Feds had given ten of thousands of **free scholarships** to our brightest youths for University study. The population overall was getting a decent education. With these measures, and lots of others, many of our **larrikin traits** were becoming less obvious.

Some, though, persisted. It took quite a few years to educate our men away from pig-swill conditions in our pubs. Shoulder to shoulder drinking after work was a tradition that was slow to die. Most pubs could add to this the attraction of a few fights between patrons on a Friday and Saturday nights. Such relics from our colonial past were not **all** gone.

Another example of contempt for authority was seen in out attitude to matters of the road. Many of our drivers, especially our country cousins, were unlicensed. The same was true for motor bikes. Rear tail lights were often missing, and brakes seen to be optional, and silent cops were the ultimate target for marauding hoons. In short, the traffic authorities had a big job policing the growing number of vehicles on the road.

So when Governments started talking about breath testing of drivers, and using the results as evidence in courts, the attitude of the man in the car was negative. Some of you will remember that initially the acceptable level of alcohol in the bloodstream was quite high, and over the years it has been lowered to the current tough levels. At the time, though, **any** set level was seen to be highly objectionable.

So arguments against the proposed measure proliferated. "They can bring out as many statistics as they like, but they have no right to interfere with **the basic Australian right to get drunk** and drive home at the weekend."

The first example below is one of the more moderate. The second shows that larrikinism is not dead.

Letters, J Ayling. The Breathalyzer amendments to the Motor Traffic Act raise important questions when considered in the light of the ideals and aims of British justice. Irrespective of their expediency in view of the road toll, let us not forget this new law violates at least two concepts of natural justice which we, as free people, ought to hold dear.

The arbitrary limit on blood-alcohol level is a legality not directly related to a driver's consumption or capacity. External symptoms, if any, may vary; thus a man cannot know without doubt whether he is committing any offence. Accordingly he may be guilty without being aware of his own guilt. The essential element of *mens rea* - guilty mind - is or may be excluded from the offence altogether.

More important perhaps is the blow that this legislation has dealt to a cherished belief - that despite our lack in this country of constitutional safeguards, no man can by law be put into a position where he is forced under penalty to incriminate himself. The amendments make it an offence to refuse a blood-alcohol test. The punishment is quite severe.

Our law and its ideals have taken more than a thousand years to develop. It is tragic that we can without public and judicial protest sweep away two of the most essential and hard-won of those ideals on the bare ground of expediency.

Letter, Mark Arthur. I am a hard-working electrician with a good family. I work six days a week, and have a round of schooners every Friday night with seven other ex-Diggers. We harm no one, and I drive a mile home.

I have been doing this for twenty years, and have only had two accidents on the way home. Both of these were caused by taking aspirin which made me drowsy.

Now, they tell me, politicians will bring in laws that say that if I have an accident on the way home, they will take me to Court, and I will lose my licence and my livelihood.

In view of my good driving record, surely there is a way to keep that in mind and leave me free to look after my family.

Comment. The legislation passed in all States, and was strengthened over the years. The results, in reduction of road deaths, speak for themselves.

NUDE FEET

Letters, Pat Carr. Perhaps someone might satisfy my curiosity as to the reason people are refused entry to Sydney's Public Library if they are not wearing footwear of some sort. It would be silly (but typical) to claim feet are dirtier than shoes. Perhaps officialdom is intent on preserving a certain amount of decorum within the walls. Surely such a suggestion is contrary to the very purpose of a library, which should be a service to users such that it can be an effective tool for their use. As such, it is basic to its usefulness that it be as functional as possible for the greatest number. How can its use by barefooted people diminish this? Next time I go to the library, I'll wear my dinner suit.

Comment. This Letter was followed up by long and deep discussions on the beauty of running barefoot through forests and tip-toeing through the tulips. It started me thinking about my early childhood, living in a small coal-mining village, and the fact that all the children there went to school every day without shoes. Rain or frost, summer and winter, over rocks and prickles in the grass, never a shoe. Most of the men would go to the butchers without shoes. At weekends, women would paddle round the house for two days without.

Attitudes had changed by 2019. There were obviously a few rebels who would approach a library with a chip on their shoulder, but most people had decided that there was **greater safety when shod**. Not only that, people now had cars, and were no longer stuck in a small and safe village community. Who would want to be seen in the big, sophisticated world without proper cladding.

In 2019, of course, the naked foot has almost disappeared. You never now see bare-footed youngsters kicking a football on an oval. You can occasionally see a shoe-less specimen near a beach or sailing on a lake. But generally, through the effects of marketing, and of Occupational Health rules, and of fashion demands, such sightings are rare. **So we can add the wearing of shoes as one of signs that the now-world is a better place.**

I must admit, though, that I am not **fully** converted. Sometimes I actually wander to the bathroom without slippers. **What a daredevil!   What a thrill!**

LIGHT THOUGHTS ON CRICKET

Letters, Frank Biddle. It is with deep regret, as a lover of true, clean sport, to note that for the first time in the history of Test cricket in this State one of the series has included Sunday as one of the days for play.

That great stalwart of English cricket, J B Hobbs, would not play on Sunday, nor, of course, the brilliant C Sindd, and I have reason to believe that our own champion of Test cricket, Donald Bradman, and also Brian Booth, are in this category.

In his book "Parson's Pitch," the Rev David Sheppard, who not so long ago visited Australia as a member of the MCC team, says: "While I was playing cricket six days a week, the fact that I kept Sunday as a different day, when I could unhurriedly turn my mind to God, was the most important single factor in keeping my faith strong."

Comment. Since WWII, religion had been under attack. Church attendances were down, and sermons were criticised for lack of pertinence in the modern world. Families praying together at night were almost unheard of, large towns no longer allowed the tolling of the Angelus from belfries, some Catholics were eating meat of Fridays. Every where you looked, organised religion was in retreat.

Even the sanctity of the Sabbath was giving way to public sport. The pre-war idea was that Sundays should be days of prayer and contemplation of devout matters, and days to retreat and think about the serious things in life. But this idea was challenged by the growing influence of sports.

Sportsmen at first were of the mind that they could go to Church on Sundays, and still play sport in the afternoon. Then they argued that there was nothing wrong with sport, indeed is should be seen as a social good. And later, some even argued that there was no need to go to Church at all.

Now, all of this blasphemy had come to the point where the institution of cricket, Australia's second religion, was talking about playing a Test match on Sundays. Oh No! Surely not. God will roll over in his grave.

MARCH NEWS ITEMS

A British-French consortium has launched the first **supersonic aircraft** created in the Western world. The **droop-nosed** *Concorde* set off on its maiden voyage from London to New York and is capable of flying at 1,450 miles per hour. It will **halve the flying time**....

The Russians **had already flown their own version of the plane,** TU144, the previous Christmas.

A major split was developing between the **Russian and the Chinese Communist Parties**. It is reported that workers in Beijing demonstrated carrying signs saying *HANG KOSYGIN,* the Russian President. These reports came from America, so it is hard to know if they are accurate ....

Still, the two Parties **were** at logger-heads with each other, and over the next few years they **did** have **a major split which persisted**, off and on, until the present day.

The Russian Embassy in Brisbane was attacked at 3 a.m. by the exploding of a series of petrol bombs that burned part of a screening front hedge. Police estimate that, had there been any wind, **the entire Lodge would have gone up in flames**. The Prime Minister apologised and our nation is red-faced. *Not in Australia* **is the dominant thought.**

Good news and bad news. Ten doctors in Sydney were working full-time in Sydney performing **illegal** abortions. Another 18 were working part time....

On the other hand, the **number of deaths in hospitals** from the effects of illegal abortions had dropped significantly over the last few years....

Apparently, **women were now using illegal doctors rather than backyard operators with their "teaspoon in a garage".** And more illegal doctors were available through word-of-mouth and they were using **scientific and sanitary methods.** Hence the drop in hospital admissions.

Supporters of the Vietnamese war had a lot of explaining to do. South Vietnam soldiers laid a mine field in the approaches to a village. A jeep-load of Australians, not knowing this, entered the minefield and detonated some mines. Then South Vietnam soldiers open fired on them. **Three Australian soldiers were killed, and five wounded....**

This is the fourth incident involving friendly fire on Australian troops. Families throughout the nation increasingly **asked why we were in Vietnam being killed by our own Allies.**

Planners in Canberra now want **the National Art Gallery** to be located on the shores of Lake Burley Griffin. This site has become available because **the projected new Parliament House** will now be built elsewhere.

The last **bachelor Beatle** has been married. Paul McCartney wedded Linda, a divorced mother with a six-year-old daughter, at a Registry Office in London. **Screaming, hysterical crowds greeted him.**

BLAST YOUR OWN HARBOUR

Project Plowhare was the brainchild of the US Government. It sought to use the power of atomic energy to peacefully benefit mankind. It did this by firing 31 nuclear warheads at 27 sites around the world. Its logic was that if excavation was needed to build a site, then a controlled nuclear explosion could be the best way to do this.

One idea that was considered was the widening of the Panama Canal. **Another** was the creation of a harbour for shipping in the Australian region of Cape Keraudren. This was on the north western coastline of Australia, basically on barren land, and relatively adjacent to Broome.

The basis was that the Cape had a huge tidal run twice a day, and went inland for miles. If a blast made a big hole in the earth, a lip could be put at the entrance to the Cape, and that would create a pond that could be used as a deep harbour. As the tidal flow came and went, the ships could come in and out over the lip. And thus a working harbour could be created.

The Letter below is typical of the support for this proposal.

Letters, Kelvin Green. While one can respect the concern of biologists for the ecology of Cape Keraudren during a nuclear blasting program, their fears are groundless. **There is simply no ecology there.**

Having been along that part of the north-west coast while pearl-fishing, years ago, I was struck by the aptness of the popular marine biologists' description of such areas as "marine deserts." One could troll a line there for hours without getting a bite. When the tide went out, all we could find were a few pearl oysters - not many - and some whiting, in the residual pools, and a few little crabs. Beach-combing there was rather unprofitable.

The great tides there, 20 to 30 feet, receded until the water line was miles out. Wool-carrying ships used to sit on the exposed sea floor and the wool wagons used to come out over the beach to the ships' sides to load their wool. Not so far from there, at Broome, the big coastal ships still lie on the bare sea floor alongside the jetty to discharge and take on cargo.

At full tide, there were some dugongs and turtles that came up close to the beach but at ebb of tide they all went out to sea. It is obvious nuclear blasting detonated at low tide there will have no effect at all on the marine ecology.

One professor referred to radio-active debris. It has been the deliberate study of Operation Plowshare to see that there is no radio-active debris released into the atmosphere. On one occasion some did escape though the cracked ground - not much - but it is hardly fair therefore to shun all underground nuclear blasting for all time and condemn the research of Operation Plowshare. It is a new kind of engineering.

It is bound to have some corners to be rubbed off; so did Nobel's Oil, many years ago, until he developed dynamite out of it. The great cost of nuclear blasting, however, has compelled a far more careful assessment of results than Nobel ever bothered to make, or needed to. It is now time to put nuclear blasting to work of a practical rather than experimental nature. Cape Keraudren is certainly a place of all places to start such tasks. There is no harbour within scores of miles of it and that coast is desolate; it needs such harbours.

Australians were not at all supportive of this. This nation had not long ago been the site of British rocket and nuclear testing at desert sites ranging from Woomera to the North West Cape. These had raised great anxiety about the immediate effects on the Aboriginal people in the regions, and about the now-apparent effects that radiation could have on them. There were currently many legal claims before the Courts over the British tests, and in fact a lot many of them lasted until the 1980's.

There were other arguments against it all. In the projects that Plowshare had already completed, with only small success, there was still the lingering fear that radiation would become apparent. Also, there was no immediate need for an expanded harbour on the North West coast.

Then again, the emerging environmental lobby in Australia were aghast at the suggestion. Mr Green's above arguments were scarcely convincing. And what about the cyclones that the Cape suffered each year. Would the new harbour, and its ships, survive tides that were twice the normal, and weather that was hugely destructive.

In all, the project got almost no local support. It was ditched. The whole Plowshare experiment was also ditched in 1977. There were few mourners at its demise.

ASIA MIGHT GET ON THE MAP

The study of languages at schools and university here was centred on Europe. Year after year, thousands of students took French, German, Italian and Latin exams in their final school exams, and a few of them trundled off to study the same subject at university.

Australia was open to criticism for this. By now, there was a considerable flow of people from here to nearby Asia. But we had no knowledge of their languages. It seemed likely that we could communicate with Asians **only** if we used interpretors. So here was one argument for the increased teaching of Asian in our institutions.

A second issue was that we had no idea of their culture or religion or history. Without these, we could perhaps function at a superficial level, but we could have no real understanding of what makes them tick and what they were feeling and thinking.

So, in an enterprising move, the school authorities in NSW, and other States, were introducing some measures to redress this. The Letter below gives some comments on the progress being made. As you will this progress was limited, but promising.

Letters, Lex Halliday. It would seem that Frederick Aarons is unaware that the areas of Asian study he advocates - ethnology, culture, etc. - are in fact minutely covered in the Education Department's new Asian Social Studies syllabus. Moreover it is vitally concerned with attitudes - and I quote - "to stimulate an interest in, and appreciation of, the religions and philosophies of Asia and a recognition that there are other value-systems and aesthetic standards besides one's own."

Next to visiting an Asian country - and even then - a study of its language is the quickest way to an understanding. All the English textbooks on "ethnology, social and political development" will not convey the attitudes of these peoples implicit for example in the nuances of their many simple forms of greeting.

Unlike the French or German, Asian attitudes are so foreign to most of us that an early familiarity with their language-forms is essential for any Asian studies. All that parents like myself ask is that this gap in an otherwise excellent course be filled; that Bahasa Indonesian and Japanese be treated on parity with French and German - that is, introduced at second-year level instead of fifth, and as qualifying subjects for the School Certificate.

Furthermore, Asian studies are attracting the "blue ribbon" students in all schools that have introduced the new syllabus. This potential university material might well make more economic use of an Asian language than does the broad spectrum of French and German students at present.

The Education Department's Seminar for Asian Social Studies, attended last Saturday by over 100 teachers of the subject from Government and non-Government schools, was evidence of the keen and intelligent interest in this vital subject. The only pity, as some speakers pointed out, was the lack of continuation of the syllabus through fifth and sixth years to university level.

Introduce Asian languages earlier, extend the course to the sixth year, give it a status that will encourage the exchange of our teachers and students with their Asian counterparts and we will have adapted - effectively - the European-orientated educational system which to date we have merely adopted.

Comment. Over the years, the fact that we live in Asia has been slowly and widely accepted, and if you look at certain suburbs in the major cities, you might think that it is the white Australians who were in the minority.

EDUCATION IN SCHOOLS

Ever since the beginning of time, and before that it seems, the provision of State education has been contentious. In Britain, political and religious fights over education have always been providing good news stories. We in Australia inherited our schools systems from Britain, and with this, of course, came the strife that has plagued education in Britain for many decades.

For Australia, I will not try to summarise all the education matters that are contentious, but will let two Letter writers do that job for me.

Letters, E Curry. About the current crisis in education:

* I hate teaching over-sized classes.

* I hate seeing pupils abandoned to conditions which were obsolete in 1900.

* I hate Federal Governments that hold out on

adequate finances for education.

* I hate State Governments that break promises and deliberately gloss over their own shortcomings.

* I hate politicians of all colours who use State aid as a potential vote-catcher.

* I hate teachers who, either through apathy or personal ambition, are lukewarm about direct action.

* I hate newspapers that admit the need for education reform, but sanctimoniously oppose direct action.

* I hate the general attitude of citizens of "The Drugged Country" that says "Give them time. After all, when we were young...!"

* Most of all I hate my Teachers' Federation for playing it ever-so-smoothly and myself for bothering to still care.

Letters, Phillip Morrissey, Association for Educational Freedom. It would seem that Messrs Wilkins and McPherson are convinced that all our education problems would be solved by a Governmental inquiry into all aspects of education. Considering the fate of so many Government inquiries, for example the Martin Report, which was quietly shelved, one finds this surprising.

Surely what is needed is for far more money to be spent immediately on education so that all our schools, both Government and Independent, could give our children the education they deserve. The need is urgent in all schools admittedly but particularly in the parochial schools, which are being paralysed for want of finance.

Despite the extraordinary use of figures by Mr Wilkins to make it appear that the Independent schools are getting the greatest share of Government handouts for education, the real facts of course are clear. It costs the Government in round figures $300 a year to educate a child in a State school, whereas the total Government grants to Independent school children amount to about $30 a year - hardly equitable.

By all means let us have an inquiry into education but' in the meantime, congratulations to Whitlam for his proposal for an immediate grant of hard cash to further improve the excellent State school system and to save the Independent schools from impending collapse. It should be remembered that Australia is desperately short of education resources and that approximately 25 per cent of these resources are to be found in the Independent schools. So to pursue policies that will slowly suffocate these schools will be disastrous for the welfare of our country.

Comment. Four of the points raised need expansion.

The first point. The State school system had been operation since before Federation, and the Catholics had run their own system separately. They had about one quarter of the total enrolments. Catholics had to fund this themselves, and their argument persisted that they paid their taxes like everyone else, and should get their eduction paid for, like everyone else.

The argument against this was that they were able to attend State schools, for free, but if they wanted a special secular education, they should pay for it themselves.

Now, Bob Menzies, in his determination to raise the standard of education in Australia, wanted to provide some funding to Catholic schools, with the expectation that buildings and facilities could be raised to the same level as in the State schools. His proposals were highly contentious, and brought the level of debate on education to fever pitch.

The second point worthy of mention is that the employment of casual teachers was in fact opposed by the Teachers Federation itself. If retired teachers were allowed back as casuals, the supply of teachers overall would have been increased a lot. That **would have reduced the bargaining power of the Federation**. This was one variation on the Closed Shop situation that be-devilled other industries.

A third point is the reference to **direct action. That means strike action.** Apparently he wanted teachers to go on strike and walk off the job at the drop of a hat, as was done by other Unions at the time. This idea was unlikely to gain much traction amongst responsible teachers.

The fourth point, referring to the use of casual teachers, is answered by the NSW Director General of Education.

Letters, D Verco, Director-General of Education.
In Letters to the Editor, Casual Teacher asks "Why cannot teachers be employed on a part-time basis by the NSW Education Department?"

Part-time employment is in fact used extensively to meet the staffing needs of our schools. When the allocation of duties in a school leaves an excess of teaching periods not requiring provision of a teacher full-time, then a casual teacher is appointed for part-time duty.

Employment of part-time casual teachers is done in a variety of ways to suit the convenience of the person appointed and the needs of the school. It may be arranged as, say, two days per week on Tuesdays and Fridays or perhaps as five mornings per week.

In most cases, however, the organisation of a school would be such as to ensure, as far as possible, that the same teacher took a class for all periods allocated to a particular subject. Again, it is not unusual to have a teacher employed full-time but with teaching commitments in two different schools.

Finally, Casual Teacher in proposing that two teachers be employed in the same school as part-time casuals to do the work of one full-time teacher is apparently unaware that this arrangement is already in use; I have no doubt that the same technique will continue to be used in the future whenever it can provide the solution to a staffing problem.

Comment. Looking back from 2019, it is obvious that a lot has not changed much. Though, I admit, a lot **has** changed.

BIG MOVES IN EDUCATION

I will return for a while to talk about Commonwealth Scholarships. These were part of the strategy that the new Prime Minister Bob Menzies started in 1951. He was prompted by the USA and Brits who were keeping Australia from being given the secrets of the atom bomb. They argued that Australia did not have the educated scientists to be let loose on the secret information involved. So Menzies had the knee-jerk reaction of giving scholarships to train hundreds of scientists.

But he went further than that. He had been a very successful University graduate, and wanted to see the nation lift its educational game, So, he funded education nation-wide, and gave institutions of learning support at all levels.

Comment. To me, this period from 1951 to 1970 was a very significant one for Australia. Menzies' effort in education changed us from a nation of low-brows on to a nation of the middle class.

Second personal comment. I had the benefit of a Commonwealth Scholarship. Without it, I would probably have ended up working in the pits all my life, like my father and brother. Both of these died at the age of 65 from dust on their lungs.

Third comment. Talk about **glass** ceilings. These dear old buggers had **anthracite** ceilings every day of their working lives.

PLEA FOR LEGALISED ABORTION

Despite the wide acceptance of the Pill among many non-Catholics and other religious, call for the legalisation of abortion continued undiminished.

Letters, Renate Cowan. I compliment the *SMH* on the editorial "Mother's Choice", urging the use of contraception instead of liberalising abortion laws. The termination of a pregnancy is, in the final analysis, nothing less than the wilful destruction of a human life and the thought of the frivolous use (or abuse) of abortion, as now practised in England, is quite nauseating.

The new law in England makes abortion legal where there is reason to believe that the child will be born mentally or physically handicapped. We should introduce this law without delay.

I know that this is a political hot potato, but I would urge all those who refer to this type of therapeutic abortion as murder to spend some time in an institution for handicapped children, trying to put themselves into the places of those condemned to a twilight existence until the day they die. What must it feel like to be tied to a wheelchair day after day, year after year, frequently in pain, often unable to speak properly, sometimes deaf or blind, dependent for all your needs on the kindness of others, stared at in idle curiosity or embarrassed pity? How much worse, when your mind is completely lucid and you know that this is literally a life-sentence with no remission for good behaviour?

Surely, a mother faced **with the possibility of having a child like this should be able to have a legal termination of pregnancy**, if she so desires, without being condemned by State or Church.

Comment. Society, in most States, was not ready for legalisation, and would not be for decades. **But see the moves in South Australia later in this book.**

APRIL NEWS ITEMS

There is a new type of dispute on the wharves. The first all-container ship has arrived in Perth from England. Dock clerks have gone on strike over issues concerning the checking of cargo. As more container ships arrive, they will in fact be met by other disputes....

The Waterside Workers Federation could see that considerable numbers of **their workers would lose jobs under containerisation**. It realised that **it could not stand in the way of** a world-wide movement. But it **could delay the evil day**, and **could extract benefits** by striking wherever it could find a dispute. **Hence this initial strike.**

The number of US military killed so far in Vietnam totals 33,700. 14 per cent of these were negroes....

Australia's dead so far totalled 267. 1,213 were wounded. These figures were greater than for the **whole** Korean war. **These were some of the costs of the war. No one has yet tabulated the benefits.**

The last book written by D'Arcy Niland **has been refused transmission by post by the Post Master General.** It contains one **four-letter word** on Page 163. Its title is *Dead Men Running*....

Australia had long been recognised by the rest of the world as having **the most capricious and stupid censorship rules**. Various authorities had confounded experts and traders and readers by **their antiquated and moralistic banning of books**....

This was the first time, however, that the all-powerful **PMG** had thrust its wisdom on to the Australian public.

A sad day for older cricket fans. Leslie Fleetwood-Smith, a famous Australian pre-war test cricketer, **was before the Court on a charge of vagrancy and alcoholism**. He was given a one-year bond, and released to the care of a Clinic. **Friends and admirers are rallying round to give him tangible support.**

Dr Jim Cairns, once a policeman and now a Labor politician, **was charged by police for handing out pamphlets** in a public street. Soon to become the Deputy Leader of the Labor Party, he had a large following, and was not shy of selling himself to the public....

He and some followers had pre-arranged a demonstration in Melbourne and **handed out pamphlets** that criticised the law against the handing-out of pamphlets. The police had been duly notified of the demonstration, and also the Press, and a crowd of 200 supporters gathered....

The charge against him was that he refused to give a Constable his name and address. **In true martyr fashion,** he proclaimed he was prepared to refuse to pay his fines, and go to jail. **But somewhat less nobly**, he limply added that this was on the proviso **that it would not affect his position in Parliament**.

Boris Karloff, the man of horror in a dozen Hollywood movies, has died. He was famous for his terrifying roles in **B-Grade Saturday afternoon movies that kept a generation of children sleepless for nights thereafter.**

THE DANGERS OF HOUSIE HOUSIE

The Chief Secretary in each State (formerly the Colonial Secretary) had a long tradition of being extremely conservative. Over the decades, no matter who the person was that occupied such a position, he seemed to be against any changes or progress.

In 1969, in NSW, he had responsibility for gaming, racing and betting. This enabled him to ignore the huge mount of illegal SP betting that was still happening in the State, and concentrate his restrictive activities on major vices such as raffles and housie-housie. He did that with fervour.

For example, any Church, sporting club, or hospital that wanted **to run a raffle had to apply to him for permission**. So too for Friday night chook raffles in the local pub. Given that he was in Sydney, and protected by a large bureaucracy, this rule was largely ignored. But prosecutions for ignoring it were still launched.

But the society-threatening vice of Housie Housie also caught his eye, as the Letter below testifies.

Letters, A Forshaw, Cronulla Working Men's Club. It came as a great shock to the many "housie" players, the charities assisted, and the club movement, to learn that Mr Willis, NSW Chief Secretary, has decided to cancel or not renew the permits **to play housie in licensed clubs**.

My Club has provided housie each Monday. The player paid 20 cents for which he received two cards in each game played (average games played were 15). The prizes and any other expenses are met by the club. The 20 cents donation went to the Sutherland District Geriatric Centre and over $1,400 has been donated since July.

We believe that we are providing a social outlet in a congenial atmosphere for many of our senior citizens and retired residents at a nominal donation of 20 cents.

Is Mr Willis able to tell us when his Government will be able to build a geriatric centre at Sutherland Hospital? Who is going to help if he will not allow us to conduct "housie"? Does Mr Willis expect senior citizens to sit on hard seats in cold halls to try to raise the necessary finance?

We hope the Chief Secretary will examine the question more closely and reverse his decision.

There were others, though, who supported the Secretary's move.

Letters, W Camden. All thinking members of the community must surely be delighted by the wisdom shown in the Chief Secretary's decision to ban games of housie-housie from licensed premises.

Too long this evil has flourished unattended in the friendly atmosphere of the club. Men and sometimes even women, too, befuddled with liquor, have readily fallen prey to the temptation to the gamble that housie-housie presents. Although they may only pay 20 cents a time, if at the end of the evening they have not won a jackpot, some people have been know to finish up as much as $10 or even $20 down.

As the Chief Secretary so clearly appreciates, drinking and gambling just do not mix. The reform so courageously taken in this case is indeed long overdue.

But there was more to be said.

Letters, L Mason. With reference to the letter from W Camden, I, as a "thinking member of the community," consider that he wants to get "with it" before making claims that men and sometimes even women too, befuddled with liquor, have readily fallen prey to the temptation to the gamble that housie presents and have been know to finish up as much as $10 or even $20 down.

The Bronte Branch of Red Cross has been privileged to conduct a housie night at the Randwick Legion Ex-Service Club for the past six months where fifteen games are played at 1 cent a card, the club providing free of cost all prizes, and the workers from Red Cross giving their services entirely free including any out-of-pocket expenses in the way of travelling.

If an evening's entertainment is provided for an outlay of 30 cents which includes a cup of tea or coffee and biscuits donated by the club's ladies' auxiliary, I fail to see how this can be classed as a "gamble that housie presents."

I am sure that W Camden has not visited housie games conducted by such licensed clubs as the above in comparison with the highly organised housie nights in halls, where it can cost players anything from $3 to $6 a night (quite out of reach for pensioners) where the whole proceeds do not go to recognised charities.

If he had, he would see the marked difference between a highly organised gambling business in the halls, and a night of relaxation for the older folk at a cost within their means and at the same time contributing 100 per cent to the Red Cross, a society that supplies so many needs to so many people irrespective of colour, class or creed.

Comment. Maybe it was only in the public halls of suburbia that there was great vice, and the great wealth of the elderly was extracted. Maybe the licensed clubs were innocent after all.

Second comment. It appears that, due to the Secretary's persistent cracking down on these weaknesses, society was able to survive until 1975.

Then the position of Chief Secretary was abolished. It was occasionally revived after that until 1995, when it disappeared for good.

SUNDAY DRINKING

Drinking laws and conditions around Australia had changed a lot from the pig-swill of twenty-five years earlier. For example, (and allowing for difference between the States) beer was now plentiful, hotels were open until about 10 o'clock at night, and there were plenty of RSL, Workers, and sporting clubs that offered reasonable amenities. A night-time entertainment industry was growing up in some States, and some pubs here and there were offering counter lunches or meals at night. Having a quiet drink at a water-hole, as opposed to getting drunk, was becoming a possibility.

There were still, however, restraints that rankled some people. In NSW if you wanted an alcoholic drink on Sundays, you could get one by driving 30 miles from your habitat, stop at a pub, sign in to say you had travelled 30 miles, drink yourself rotten, and drive home full as a bull. But you could not buy a drink at the local pub.

So, agitation was growing for Sunday drinking laws to be changed.

Letters, Heinz Bernhard. Apart from all the sanctimonious and bigoted objections by Sabbatarians of all creeds, the main argument against legislating for hotels to open on Sundays is that it will lead to a greater consumption of alcohol and thus to more accidents and deaths on the roads.

This devious kind of reasoning seems to be the least valid one. On the contrary, every Sunday you may observe an eager exodus of thirsty imbibers scurrying along the main roads and expressways to take them beyond the statutory 30 miles, where the law, since the days of the bushrangers and of Cobb and Co coaches, allows them to wash the dust of the dirt and gravel road from their parched throats.

All the travel-weary Sunday drivers on the Windsor or Wiseman's or Wollongong Road has to do is sign his name in the visitors' book of the village hostelry or inn, and he may fill himself up with the proverbial "one for the road" until he is unfit to drive his vehicle home without endangering his passengers, other road users and least of all himself, whereas the more sensible horse and his cart of older days could proceed with safety on their dusty journey.

If we allow the companionable and compulsive pub-crawler to walk just round the corner to "the local" all through the weekend, we shall make the roads safer for the Sunday sports fan and the short distance picnicker with his cans of beer rattling in the boot of his car.

Besides he can always go to his club - sports, professional and even the denominational ones - which will not voluntarily forfeit their legal rights to open for trade on a Sunday by objecting conscientiously.

The writer got quite a few responses. One writer thinks that Sunday should be a day for family and church.

Not everyone agrees with her.

Letters, Ann Phillis. Nola Johnson sees the entire world from the inside of her tiny church. A day in the country, with two dozen friends, and all of the kids, is a wonderful family day. Most people drink and drive responsibly on such days.

The exceptions are the young people who drink and drive like maniacs, with or without liquor. I would like Nola Johnson to say **openly** that she is against drink any where at any time, and not to clothe her objection behind a cloak of sanctimonious concern for public safety.

Other Letters push different views.

Letters, Ernest Vines. Heinz Berhnard seems to believe that a greater consumption of alcohol will not lead to more accidents and deaths on the roads. Most reasonable and fair-minded people will probably heartily disagree with him.

The number of cars that gather near every pub **during the week** is a fair indication of what will happen **on Sundays** if Sunday drinking in public houses is allowed. With drinking allowed in pubs all day on Sundays, what will the home-coming be like?

Letters, J Leslie. From the bastions of their churches and homes, the clerics and the housewives are proposing to join forces against lawful Sunday drinking reform.

Surely the clergy don't think that Sunday opening will make people less pious! Countries far richer in religious symbolism and practice than Australia, such as Ireland, Bavaria and Italy, have Sunday opening.

Must it for ever remain a part of the **great Australian loneliness** for bored tourists and New Australians to wander our lifeless and dull cities on Sundays? **This loneliness has driven not a few New Australians to suicide.** Contrast the happy relaxed atmosphere of European cities on Sundays, enjoyed by citizen and tourist alike, with their licensed facilities.

From my observations, more alcoholics derive

from lonely rooms and apartments than ever do from the social drinking in hotels and clubs.

Letters, A Vatseas. Without wishing to enter the controversy on the move to open hotels on Sunday, I feel I must challenge the assumption of J Leslie that lack of such facilities has contributed to the "loneliness that has driven not a few New Australians to suicide."

The loneliness and homesickness of New Australians is aggravated not by the absence of limitless bacchanalia around them, but by the abuse and derogatory remarks slung at them by Australians affected by liquor.

Theirs is not the kind of loneliness to vanish at the sight of Sunday throngs in and out of hotel bars with beer taps kept running. New Australians generally dread the introduction of schemes likely to increase alcohol consumption. They know too well the difference between meeting a sober Australian and trying to avoid a drunken one.

To say that Sunday hotel trading will brighten their lives is too flippant and ludicrous.

Comment. Sunday trading was introduced in all States over the next few years. Country pubs suffered a lot. As it turned out, the picnic in the country, talked about above, did not convert into picnics at the local pub, so alcohol consumption remained unchanged. What did happen was that Sunday openings gave birth to an industry that still delivers night-time performances by artists in local pubs. Some of our youth like this, and oldies living nearby decidedly do not.

In any case, opening on Sundays did not become a disaster.

PENSIONS IN 1969

Pensions for the elderly were being paid by the Government, but they were subject to a means test. That meant that if you had a big enough income, or held fairly large assets, you did not get the full pension.

This is very much like it is today.

And as I look back at my 1949 book, the situation in 1969 is very much like it was then. In that year, the idea of a means test on pensions was fairly new. The central argument against it was put in this Letter.

Letters, J Paoloni. As I am looking forward to becoming an old-age pensioner myself soon I would like to comment on Charmian Clift's demand that the means test be abolished. The means test is there to stop greedy people, who have plenty to live on, from getting a handout from the already meagre pension cake.

Like child endowment, to **give everybody a handout** irrespective of wealth and of income **is to sharply reduce the pension rightly due to the less fortunate.**

The often enlarged means test is liberal enough to allow a married couple a reduced pension, and full pension benefits if their assets do not exceed $20,319.

The oft-quoted argument that one has always paid taxes and therefore one is entitled to a pension does not hold water. The average worker has made **a greater sacrifice in paying his taxes** than have his wealthy counterparts who obviously have enough.

I agree that a special contributory scheme based on income could be evolved in this country. At present England and New Zealand are groaning under the weight of subsidising the well-off.

Comment. But this Letter was not from 1949. It was written in April this year, 1969. The argument, and the situation, had not changed **in twenty years.**

But more interesting, **in 2019, the central argument still has not changed.** Should someone who has not saved for their retirement get a pension, while someone who has worked and saved diligently gets none? Or, put another way, if there is a limited pie to share, should it go to those who have income and assets, or to those who have neither?

My own answer, when I looked at this question in 1949, was that it was too hard for me. I asked readers to make up their own minds. This time, for 1969 (and 2019), I have thought about it again, and now my answer is that, if we put our own situations aside, there is no answer to this question. No matter what you say, you will be criticised, and rightly so. There just is no defensible answer.

MAY NEWS ITEMS

The Prime Minister John Gorton says that **our National Anthem is *God Save The Queen*.** It should be played on all occasions involving the monarch, or the Governor General, or "regal but not gala functions"....

However, ***Waltzing Matilda*** was also acceptable. Indeed it **"is our national song"**. It should be played on such occasions as honouring our athletes or at non-State functions attended by our Prime Minister....

He is not contemplating the writing on a new anthem. **No mention was made of *Advance Australia Fair*.**

Sir Paul Hasluck, was sworn in as our new Governor General. This post is often seen as just a ceremonial office. But the GG did have **to earn his keep a few years later when he dismissed Gough Whitlam.**

The war against conscientious objectors rages on. The Australian Government says that a sincere objector can be excused if he objects to **all** wars. But **if he objects to a particular war (such as Vietnam**), then he is committing **a political act, and will go to prison....**

The Australian Council of Churches has **changed its position** and says that it now supports **all** sincere objectors. The Churches argue that a person may or may not have certain political views, but **he may sincerely object to killing enemy combatants regardless of his political views....**

The Government remained unmoved.

A 30-year-old Irishman told a priest at Sydney's Catholic Cathedral that **he planned to kill the Archbishop**, Cardinal Gilroy. He had with him **a loaded shotgun**, and plenty of ammunition. The priest alerted the police and the man was arrested and sent to a psychiatric hospital.

The Pope removed a 1,900-year-old order that said that women attending church must cover their heads.

In Los Angeles, **Dame Zara Holt**, the widow of the deceased former Prime Minister Harold Holt, **was invited to launch** a US destroyer named after Holt....

She took the customary bottle of champagne and bashed against the hull, but it remained in one piece. She and her female companion tried again, but once more failed. In fact, it took **eight attempts before it shattered**, and then only with the help of the manager of the shipyard....

A LA Newspaper celebrated the event with the headline **"Aussie women too weak to break a bottle"**.

The Federal Government has announced that it is likely to build a nuclear power plant on the NSW coast soon. It will generate electricity for most of NSW....

It is suggested that Australia could have 10 such plants within 10 years. One perceived advantage of the scheme is that it would be easy to switch reactors to produce Uranium 239 for making H-bombs....

"Over my dead body", said thousands of objectors. None of the reactors were ever built.

A BRIEF LOOK AT VIETNAM OPINION

Of course the war in Vietnam was grinding on. It seemed that public opinion was slowly swinging against it, but was still about 55 per cent against and 45 per cent for.

This writer below, in a matter-of-fact manner, raises a spectre that not many people had thought of. He talks of the possibility that the war could go on for another ten years.

Letters, K Ross. Senator J Stennis, Chairman of the Armed Services Committee, says the United States military forces might still be in Vietnam in 10 years. I don't think so, and I would like to be as sure of winning the lottery as I am that the Americans will be out of Vietnam long before **1979**.

Several factors are involved. First, there is the real need for the US Administration to withdraw from some of its over-commitments around the world (this need was clearly expounded by Walter Lippmann in his last published article, printed a month or so ago in the "Herald"). Domestic conditions in the USA, and possible trouble in Latin America will influence US withdrawal trends from Asia.

"Bring the Boys Home from Asia." If this slogan would not be a winner, I would be very surprised.

Last, but not least, there's China. While China is still perhaps something of a "paper dragon," this will not always be the case. China is undoubtedly becoming more powerful militarily year by year, and there will probably come a time before 1979 when the US will have to fight a major war with

China if she wishes to stay on the mainland of Asia.

There is, I think, a real need for the US to rethink its position with regard to the Asian mainland.

Comment. There is no doubt that if the war looked like going on for another decade, public opinion would quickly see to it that Australia was no longer in it. Much support now was based on **the assumption that the war would soon end**. The longer it went on, this war, like all other wars, would become increasingly unpopular.

EXPORT OF AUSTRALIAN MERINOS

Since the 1930's, there has been talk off and on about exporting Australian merinos to overseas destinations, whenever the wool trade had a big downturn. It was not just the case of selling our wool, or our meat. It was about selling our live rams and ewes so that they could be used for breeding.

Clearly such sales would provide an income stream while ever our wool sales were down. The main objection was that if we sold the live sheep, the buyers would be able to breed. Then soon after they would have flocks of Australian sheep that they could not sell. This would drive the market price down, to the obvious detriment of our graziers. We would be, in effect, selling the farm.

1969 was a year when there was a world-wide glut in production of wool, and it was the start of a build up of a national stock-pile. This reserve was a problem for the next twenty years. The situation was made more severe by the increasing share that synthetics took of the clothing market. This was the start of a worrying period for our graziers and the wool industry.

So, once again, controversy erupted in 1969 over whether we should be selling our **live sheep** for **breeding**. I have given you the main argument **against** doing this, so now I present an advocate in favour.

Letters. B Wilson. Dr Edgar's Letter is not convincing. Australia has bred and improved its sheep for two hundred years. The merino of today is infinitely better than the merinos we originally imported. And it is better than any other in the world. We got this situation by careful breeding. We took into account weather, location, floods and droughts, Trade Union rules, distances from facilities, disease and remedies, and other factors.

This was not by chance. It happened year after year, with careful selection. We just can't hand over all of these advances as if it was just their wool we are selling.

Let me add that, if we take our merinos to other lands, they will not produce nearly as well. We are good because we are ever watchful. **Dump Australian merinos into foreign lands and they will perform as well as African elephants in our deserts.** We should forget our short-term cash flow, and think twenty years ahead.

Comment. In general, over the years, the Australian merino has not been **widely** sold overseas. **The warning given by Mr Wilson is one reason.** So too, was his injunction to remember the future. This appealed to our conservative graziers who **do** have concern for the longer term.

TOWN VERSUS GOWN

Most citizens and burghers of Sydney were happy with Sydney University. They took pride from the fact that it was world-class, they liked having the wisdom that it brought to the community, they even liked having an academic hierarchy that they could look up to, rather than to an aristocracy as in England.

What they did not like was any misbehaviour that the students committed.

An annual University festival sometimes got a little out of hand, and a few apologies were necessary to smooth ruffled feathers. The Press always played these up to the hilt, and so, about every third year, there were solemn enquiries into what had happened, and a few wrists were slapped.

In 1969, the Governor of NSW, Sir Roden Cutler, was scheduled to give a speech at the University. There was to be a little pomp for this occasion, and as part of this, the Sydney University Regiment was to parade. A group of 100 anti-Vietnam students sat down on the path the Regiment was to march, and another 200 pro-Vietnam scholars tried to remove them. So there were punch-ups and scuffles. Roden arrived in the middle of this and was abused by some of the happy unruly mob.

The Press enjoyed reporting all this. Normally, a barney at the University got their full attention, but this had the background of the war in Vietnam. So the *SMH* Editorial next day called the fighters louts and hooligans, and several commentators talked about expelling combatants from the University. Premier Askin, talking big to the Law and Order constituents, threatened to withdraw support from the University.

Roden, on the other hand, was not disturbed and saw it as part and parcel of his public duties to get roasted at times.

Letters to the Editor poured in. One gentleman came up with a list of excuses for the Anti-Vietnam group. It is a bit lengthy, but it would be a pity to omit any part of it.

Letters, Allan Ashbolt Ex-Services Human Rights Assn of Aust. It seems to me that Press and public alike should be making stronger efforts to understand the mainsprings of student revolt and agitation. These young people were born in the era of moral perplexity and vast social change that followed world War II. They see in the Nazi concentration camps and the mass annihilation of Hiroshima a logical expression of the violence inherent in Western civilisation; they see socialism in the USSR being subjugated to the demands of power politics; they see the capitalist democracies putting national strength and security before individual freedom and dignity; they see Western man everywhere trapped by an inheritance of brutality, authoritarianism, acquisitiveness and hypocrisy. Instead of retreating into cynicism, acquiescence or opportunism, they are trying, by challenging conventional institutional structures, to make an evolutionary breakthrough in human behaviour and standards.

Are they "louts" for standing up (or more precisely

in this case, sitting down) against the symbols of a social order which offers, to the young men among them, the moral alternatives of gaol or the Army? For the situation these boys confront is that, if they defy society's command to be trained in and probably to practise legalised violence against other persons, then they must submit to the humiliation of having legalised violence practised against their own persons.

Allan Ashbolt was recognised for his fervent anti-war stance. After that little diatribe, he waxes on. He concludes with the wonderful forecast that "as a result of their opposition to military conscription, they look like producing Australia's largest number of political prisoners since transportation ended."

Ashbolt did not have it all his own way.

Letters, Douglas Cohen. It is with regret and sadness that I find myself in complete agreement with the sentiments so well expressed in your editorial "Student louts": regret, because this has happened at my alma mater and sadness because there exists in our community a group who presumably should have the intelligence to know better and has such little regard for basic standards of social behaviour, for human dignity and for all those values which so many of their fathers' generation felt so strongly about that, 30 years ago, they were prepared voluntarily to suffer considerable hardship and inconvenience to uphold them.

Most members of the community, particularly if

they have any association with the university, will realise that this is only a vociferous minority. Nevertheless, it is a minority which cannot be allowed to continue to behave in this way. If these immature exhibitionists are not prepared to accept basic standards of social behaviour, the university authorities should not continue to tolerate their presence. The choice is theirs but the university authorities have a duty to see that they make this choice and abide by it.

Letters, T Handran-Smith. The student attack on Sir Roden Cutler will cause a revulsion of feeling against students, in previously tolerant citizens.

University students are expected to be radical and intolerant of authority, but society, not unreasonably, expects its young, intellectual elite to express its radical ferment with wit, intelligence and humanity.

A student body capable of such cowardly hoodlumism deserves to alienate the tolerance of all men of goodwill.

Most of the Letters were offended that an ordinary demo had deteriorated to the stage where a much-respected Governor was affronted.

Their arguments continue.

Letters, W Kuttner, Standing Committee of Convocation, University of Sydney. The graduates of the University of Sydney express publicly their disapproval and disgust at the discourtesy extended to his Excellency the Governor during his official visit to the university for the purpose of delivering the Occasional Address during the Arts graduation ceremony on May 1.

Members of the Committee, representing all the graduates of the university and thus many shades of political opinion, find no fault with the concept that freedom of expression and protest form part of, not only university life, but also of public affairs.

They do, however, completely disagree with the manner in which the protests were carried out and the discourtesy extended to our visitor. We deplore, on behalf of graduates, the incidents created by a section of an irresponsible minority of students and other agitators.

But later Letters were **more moderate and less one-sided**.

Letters, Chris Beale, Sydney University Students' Representative Council. Mr Askin's implied threats, of reducing financial aid to Sydney University if its administrators do not discipline the leaders of the demonstration involving the Governor, are somewhat rash.

While the university should discipline the leaders, Mr Askin's threats would, if carried out, hurt all 16,000 students at Sydney University.

In fact, only 100 students demonstrated against the University Regiment, about 300 students battled with the demonstrators, and 1,000 student onlookers gave three cheers and clapped the

Governor after he completed his inspection of the regiment's guard of honour.

Letters, P Yorke. Messrs Askin and Cutler's decision that they may take action against so-called radical students is an unwise one. It seems to be motivated as punishment for holding a particular political viewpoint rather than for the sake of justice.

The "louts and hooligans, "as the "Herald's" editorial terms them in last Thursday's demonstration, were not confined to the radical students nor can there be any certainty that the missiles and fruit thrown were hurled by the demonstrators.

The term "louts and hooligans" implies that students are unprincipled, while the truth is that they have too much principle. **They put their principles first**, which is a rarity in this land flowing with beer and money; usually principles take third place.

Letters, Black-eyes. I am a student at **Melbourne University**, and I am happy to report that **students there feel just as strongly about Vietnam as Sydney does**. So we have demos, and if they end up in bit of rough stuff, all the better. **We finish in the same pub chasing the same girls.**

After a few years, **we grow out of it**. Its better for society than true crime and violence.

Comment. The University did slap a few wrists, but no one felt any sting. The demo did not change any opinions, the Press continued its campaign to exploit university events, and the Premier puffed his chest and claimed credit from his Law and Order constituents.

Comment. So it appears to have served no purpose. But I think it did. It allowed people to argue over something trivial, but at the same time express their Vietnam views. These latter were being suppressed by all parties, lest their venting led to conflict and wounds that would not heal.

Because of this, the University fiasco, citizens could safely have an opinion that did not affect the life and death of their sons. Whatever the cause, citizens all over the State were adamant one way or the other and were quite lavish with their opinions. A little University demo went a long way.

MODERN ART

Modern Art was very strong in 1969. The art works of the Masters of the last millennia or so were seen to be really not much chop, and instead the squares and coloured triangles and floating eyes of drop-out kindergarten long-hairs were now the talk of the town.

You might suspect from the above that I am not a great enthusiast for this barbarity but, as usual, I will hide my contempt and not criticise these monstrosities. There is, however, at least one other person who agrees with me, and I enclose her Letter with my fulsome support.

Letters, Rita Bloomfield. There is a question a lot of people want to ask, and it is this: What has happened to all the works of art owned by the National Gallery?

We make periodical visits there and we prowl

around the jungle of geometrical designs, splodges of colour and some double-jointed object doing the splits; we fight our way clear of twisted wire and weird symbols, looking for something to rest our tortured eyes, and about all we find is a Roman marble of a youth and a dog, in the forecourt.

There are a great number of us who think this way, and we are all mighty vocal about it at home, but no one seems to want to stand up in public and call this rubbish, that we are having foisted on to us in the name of art, by its right name.

I for one would gladly see a few of Norman Lindsay's, Hilder's, Gruner's and Lambert's in their place. I would like to renew my acquaintance with "The Dancer" and Julian Ashton's portrait of Rose Scott, and Sir William Dobell's of Dame Mary Gilmore, to say nothing of Rayner Hoff's sculpture of her head, and where is Orpen's "Italian Major"?

The best thing the gallery has done for me personally over the past years, has been to move Le Duc's lifesized mare and foal into the gardens, where those who love her can go and worship in peace.

For pity's sake let us have done with this madness and whip the moneychangers out of the temple before we become a race of complete degenerates.

Comment. I must thank Rita Bloomfield for her wonderfully perceptive comments.

WALTZING MATILDA

Mr Gorton was not the only person with an opinion on our National Anthem.

Letters, M Earl. Whether the intellectuals like it or not, "Waltzing Matilda" is already our national song, if not the official anthem. It's known from Broome to Brisbane, Darwin to Perth, because it has been accepted and perpetuated by the ordinary Australian, and why not? It has a rollicking tune (no matter its origin), a tale of our forbears, both gentry and convict, and for a hero, that figure beloved of children, the swaggie.

If the psychologists put their minds to it they would no doubt find in this song reasons for some of our emerging national characteristics such as our insistence on a "fair go" for all and the right of the transport unions to strike leaving you and me stranded on the street corner.

Finally, "Waltzing Matilda" is one song when heard by Australians overseas that evokes nostalgia for sun, sand, dusty country roads and nasal voices on the neat suburban block where gumtrees do battle with telegraph poles.

Letters, H Townshend. Does Mr Gorton really want "Waltzing Matilda" as our national anthem? Surely we have more to be proud of in this wonderful country than to sing about a sheep-stealing swaggie who committed suicide!

JUNE NEWS ITEMS

A man approached the guard at **the perimeter gate at Long Bay gaol**, drew a gun, and told the guard to drop his gun belt. He did so. He was then told to walk away, He did so. When he looked back, **the man had gone. So had his gun.** The villain was never apprehended.

The Federal Government will pay **30 per cent of the wages** paid to employers who take on **Aborigines full time**. Also, for young Aborigines who move away from home seeking full time employment, **they will be paid a living allowance on top of their wages**....

This is in keeping with the Government's new policy of **reversing attitudes to Aborigines**.

In the South China sea, in bright moonlight, **a US destroyer collided with the Australian air-craft carrier,** *Melbourne*. The *Frank E Evans* was sunk, and **77 Americans are missing**....

The collision occurred five years after **the HMAS** *Voyager* **collided with the** *Melbourne*. 83 seamen were lost in that disaster.

The love-rock musical exploded onto the stage at Sydney's wildest-ever first night **presentation of** *Hair*....

"The men wore the most outrageous varieties of mod gear. They included Regency gear and **befrogged** gilded and military uniforms, sombrero hats, furs, feathers, silks, satins and brocades...."

The audience took everything in its stride. Memorable were the near-nudity, joyous shouting of four-letter words, bare-breasted dancing, and **a mass strip on stage at the end.**...

The Office of Chief Secretary of NSW was currently held by Eric Willis. Secretaries had been very priggish in the past, and fanatical about the desire **to preserve public morality.** He however commented that *Hair* was cleverly presented and quite revolutionary as a form of theatre. **What a welcome change in attitude this was.**

Edward, the Duke of Windsor who renounced the Throne, was invested as the Duke of Wales at the age of 17 in 1911. By tradition, he wore **a medieval-style dress** that included a fur-trimmed tunic and knee-length satin breeches and white stockings. "It was the most embarrassing day of my life"....

His great-nephew **Prince Charles**, aged 20, will now be invested into the same role. He gets off lightly. His regalia will be that of **the twentieth-century uniform** of the Colonel-in-Chief of the Royal Regiment of Wales.

The Queen, on the traditional day of her birthday, **created 17 new Knights.** They included airline boss, Reg Ansett, and Russell Drysdale, and A V Jennings. All of these you will recognise....

There were many, though, that you probably never heard of. Try yourself on David Brand and Cecil Looker. Justice Crisp? Henry Norman Giles? What about (now) Lady Rita Mary Buxton?

BIG CLUBS ARE TRUMPS

Over the past 15 years the States, at various times, have changed our drinking laws to allow for local communities to form Clubs, licensed to sell alcohol, that allow members to eat and drink in reasonable conditions. These were alternative venues to the grog-swilling pubs. Almost every town or suburb in the nation had such a club, and membership included over ten per cent of the adult population.

At the beginning, they were founded around existing community groups. For example, returned servicemen wanted watering holes, and found them in RSLs. Sporting clubs, including bowling clubs, and Masonic clubs, and Catholic clubs all got licences. Workers clubs were in all industrial areas.

They served their purposes at the local level. Drunkenness on the streets virtually disappeared. Families could go out at night and have a meal. Workmen could get a beer after work without the former pig-swill conditions.

Then the clubs got licences to bring in poker machines to replace the old fruit machines. The machines got faster, slicker, and played for larger sums. What a goldmine!

Now, in 1969, some clubs were starting to go past this stage and were expanding in all dimensions.

Letters, F Campbell. The State Government is to be congratulated on **its proposal to limit club membership**. That is, they want to stop big clubs from getting bigger.

Clubs are run by boards of directors who, inflated by the poker-machine bonanza of a few years ago, were lifted into the clouds and are still there in spite of the justified taxation which should have brought them down to earth.

I have no quarrel with the Taj Mahal-type premises which were erected and fittingly appointed, creating a comfortable club atmosphere in which it was possible to spend pleasant hours with club members and friends.

But what a change has taken place. Members, having woken up to the impossible odds of the poker-machines, are not prepared to pour money down their throats and, to overcome this, new members are being stacked in regardless of the comfort and convenience of members.

The atmosphere of the large clubs has changed. The Registered Clubs' Association is appealing for mercy in the name of an "industry." It surely has become an industry.

If the clubs are in trouble, the logical solution is to **adopt realistic membership subscriptions** so that the many thousands of members, who use the facilities for four or five dollars a year and refuse to be taken in by bandit poker-machines, will not be placed in the position of sponging on those who are.

The Government's proposal may have the effect of bringing boards to their senses and restoring the clubs to their original purpose.

If it does, members will be grateful to the Government and the boards may then exercise circumspection in management.

Comment. We all know that over time, some clubs have become mammoths. They have huge buildings, they control half the national teams (and their juniors) in Rugby League and Soccer, they run show-business events, and hold boxing matches in their vast auditoria. Efforts to curb them emerge at times, but the genie appears to have left the bottle.

Fortunately, not all local clubs have succumbed. In many areas, the smaller ones have folded, and now reasonable-sized clubs still meet local needs. People can get food and drink at a reasonable price, and some weekend entertainment to those patrons who are fortunate enough to be stone deaf.

Comment. In NSW, in 1953, there were 393 registered Clubs. In 1969, there are 1,446.

A SNIPPET FROM THE VIETNAM WAR

Archbishop Strong was an Anglican who had served his country well during WWII in New Guinea. He had delivered the oration at Harold Holt's funeral service, and was much respected throughout his Church and the community.

However, he got into a bit of hot water after he visited our troops in Vietnam.

Letters Carol McLean. Strong's statement, after visiting Australian Servicemen in Vietnam, that "it's rough going for some, but I think **they have all benefited from the experience**", deserves comment as he represents a very large section of the Australian Christian community.

Leaving aside the obvious fact of several hundred young men who have been killed, and the other hundreds who will carry injuries all of their lives (and it's impossible to find any "benefit" from being either dead or permanently injured), it seems terribly insensitive for a churchman to say young men can "benefit' from being involved in the organised killing of other human beings.

When we can begin to look at war realistically and not propped up and defended by such simplistic (and immoral) slogans as "better there than here," then perhaps we can admit honestly that war makes victims of our young men, and those conscripted on the other side, and the children trapped between!

CENSORSHIP DEBATE

Given the adult remarks from Eric Willis on the opening of the musical Hair, many people hoped that our puritanical obsession with protecting our citizens from schoolboy smut would have been given a rest.

But, NO! Almost immediately, the Chief Film Censor stepped in and banned the showing of a Swedish film, called *I love, you love* at the Sydney Film Festival.

I have been told that one scene in the film showed people copulating from different angles, and displaying the ridiculous expressions and emotions that seem inevitable on such occasions. No matter whether this is true or not, it showed action that was too much like real life for the censor, and he thought that Film Festival patrons would be better humans if they were saved from viewing it.

In any case, the producer of the film was told that if he
would not cut the evil scene, then the entire film would be
banned. He withdrew his entry.

As an aside, let me tell you that at the time many people
went to such Festivals for the very purpose of seeing the
lusty, "dirty", scenes that censors forbade.

Back to *I love, you love*. Many writers now vied to state their
case, sometimes **for** censorship, and sometimes **against**.

A group of 14 writers and actors, most of them well-known
to TV audiences, sent the following telegram to the Prime
Minister and to the *SMH*.

**Letters, Sue Becker, Del Cartwright, Gordon
Chater, Charmian Clift, Anne Deveson, Claire
Dunne, Pat Lovell, George Johnston, Dorothy
Pope Harry Robinson, Maggie Tabberer, Stuart
Wagstaff, Diana Ward and Bruce Webster.**

We have just sent the following telegram to the
Prime Minister, Mr John Gorton:

We strongly deplore Senator Scott's authoritarian
banning of Swedish film "I Love, You Love" on
grounds this is contrary to the entire spirit of
agreement with festival committees, and is insult
to Swedish Government, to Bjorkman, and to
adult Australian public. We also object to moral
blackmail suggesting future penalties if matter not
dropped.

The next Letter supported the Censor. I like his reference
to the dangers of following Rome.

Letters, M Hare. As a Labor supporter I must take

off my hat to Senator Scott for taking the required action to have an undesirable film banned. It is high time that parliamentarians realised that they should stick up for decency, as against decadence, in their running of the country. The inroads being made by perverts, masquerading under the names of "avant-garde" people, can be seen throughout the democratic world, and is doing democracy much more harm than Communism has ever even threatened us with.

Everyone knows what happened to Rome when its morals decayed. The same trend is being developed here by opportunist entrepreneurs. Again congratulations, Senator Scott. Your action has given a huge majority of Australian citizens fresh heart. This majority has been taking things quietly and it's about time it made itself heard.

There were plenty of other opinions.

Letters, Helen Williams and eight others. We are nine professional women - censor that first, please, Senator Scott - who wish to applaud Mr Bjorkman for his decision to withdraw his entry from the Film Festival.

It is obvious even to us innocents in the field of film censorship that if we are, as a nation, prepared not only to tolerate it, but initially to give this censorship board the power it holds, we are not ready to take our place in the world as one of the "grown-ups." If Senator Scott sees filth and perversion where none exists, let us then pity the youth of Australia, who are constantly having it pointed out to them.

For indeed, if the youth of Australia has depraved thoughts the blame lies squarely at the feet of the Censorship Board, which treats all reference to matters of a sexual nature in literature, art, films, etc., as dirty and harmful. Surely a nation of young people such as ours, gay and proud to be alive, and free to think and feel, is pure enough to see a film such as "I Love, You Love" as a genuine, sensitive approach to a problem which does exist, without wanting to rush out of the cinema and rape every pregnant woman in sight.

We have, through this and other such incidents, been placed in the humiliating position where Australia is represented abroad as a nation of ill-educated, insensitive, uncultured, immature bores - hardly the image we wish to foster in this supposedly "enlightened" age.

Letters, "Hair" Hater. Hurrah for the greatest contribution to the education of the people towards theatre and arts made in Australian history! Send up the rockets, light up the skies! Let's celebrate the coming of "Hair" with all that wondrous freedom of speech and modesty on stage. Such education! Four-letter words! Nudity! One feels overawed with the magnificence of the contribution to our way of life.

Fellow Australians, take note of those arty folk - only by such flagrant displays can you enjoy theatre! Even TV personalities are beating the drums incessantly. I wish they would shut up.

I'm sick to death hearing about how bad the censorship laws are. I'm far from being a religious crank but believe in censorship. After all, everyday laws are a form of censorship, which are needed for our survival, so that adults (able to think for themselves, you know) don't rob, steal and kill each other.

Comment. Roger Millis was a student leader when I was at Sydney University. He was a leader of the arty-crafty set, and was notable for his robust common-sense.

In a Letter, he remembered that last year Willis had banned the third segment of the play *American Hurrah* on the "complaint of an anonymous Bathurst grandmother and the advice of two Vice Squad detectives". He views with some suspicion Mr Willis' enlightenment. He hopes that Willis will confirm his conversion by placing the authority to censure in the hands of **a properly representative body rather than leave it in the hands of a single person.**

As it turned out, Millis's scepticism was justified. Censorship across this fair nation continued to be exercised by a dozen arbitrary, narrow-minded and ignorant persons for decades to come.

So the argument went on. Should we be spared from reality, or should we be glutted with it? Should sex be shrouded in the bedrooms with the lights out, or should it be a part of the world round us? Should we have a Censor who "protects" everyone or should he draw the line a bit before "everyone"? **I do not know. Do you?**

THE MAN ON THE MOON

There is a growing expectation that the US will soon put a man on the moon.

Letters, David Griffiths, aged 11 years. I read an article recently which pointed out that there are 17 million suffering refugees in the world.

It is costing America 20,000 million dollars to put a man on the moon for three days. It costs $1 to keep a refugee family alive for a week. I think the money would be far better spent helping the refugees of the world.

The first response is a predictable pat on the head for the child.

Letters, Marnie Buik. Bravo for Master David Griffiths, who thinks, as many adults do, that it is a waste to put a man on the moon.

Here is a boy with compassion, the ability to think clearly, the courage to express his thought (though it doesn't agree with most space-struck youngsters) and the drive to get it on paper. I wonder if his mother knows how lucky she is?

The second Letter is not so kind.

Letters, Keith Cairnes. Tell your 11-year-old correspondent, and those similarly depressed by the starving millions and the cost of putting man into space, to take heart. Man's uncontrollable and healthy urge to explore will lead ultimately, as it always has done, to an improved life for humanity generally.

Already we are seeing earth as it appears from 250,000 miles away and our minds are expanding. Soon the photographs and the eyes of men will expose our miserable little home globe for what it is, and from such distance that a realisation of its utter insignificance will be inescapable.

Those now too ignorant, selfish, greedy, lazy or busy to exercise their imagination or to give a human thought for their fellows will have the truth laid before them, their anthropocentric outlook will be shown for what it is worth, and will be discarded for a more sensible notion of their place in space.

Then superstition will vanish. Those awful twin diseases of the mind, racism and patriotism, will fade away and be replaced by a glorious humanism which will have no room for bigotry and religious dogma. So let's get out into space, as soon as possible, and look back.

This response repudiates the child, and instead offers us the glories that can be attained by gung-ho ventures into space. Presumably, hunger will disappear, and so too will racism and patriotism. Bigotry and religious dogma will go too. What a world!

JULY NEWS ITEMS

A 13-year-old boy in the Children's Court in Perth has been before a magistrate a number of times. He has now escaped from his detention centre and been caught stealing. The **magistrate said that the boy should be punished by a thrashing**. "there is no other way to deal with you"....

The Welfare Department has **not decided if it will carry out the decision**. It will wait for "further details". This suggests that it will not.

The Queen's son Charles was to be invested as **the Prince of Wales**. **Extremists from Wales did not like this**, and have exploded a number of bombs to protest. Security for the investiture is tight....

One of the main worries was **that marbles will be thrown under the wheels of Charles' carriage**, and they might cause the horses to stampede or shy....

Late news. This did **not** happen. Just Paper talk.

The Queen, Elizabeth II, had a different story. She arrived at Carnarvon in Wales **by Royal Train**. Just a few minutes after she left the Train, **a bomb exploded** that destroyed several metres of the track where the Train had been docked. No one was injured and a young man was taken into police custody....

Then as her carriage moved to the Castle, **a spectator threw an egg at her carriage**. He was arrested by the crowd. As he was taken away by the Police, many of the crowd **bellowed "traitor" and "lynch him"**....

Charles was invested amid all this. **Quite a day for the Royal family.** No one was lynched.

Another boy in a Perth Court was awarded small damages for an arm injury and scratches he suffered when **he entered the cage of a bear at Perth Zoo.** The event occurred five years ago, and was finally settled....

The boy's teacher had allowed the school children to wander despite her knowledge of their "mischievous propensities". The judge found that when the boy entered the cage, **he ceased to be an invitee and become a trespasser.**

The US has announced that on **or about July 16**, a rocket called *Apollo II* will launch into space and land men on the moon.

July 4th was Independence Day in the USA. **In all our major cities this year, it was a day for protesting against the Vietnam War.** Over 100 people across the nation were charged with offences committed during demonstrations in the streets.

A **former Roman Catholic priest will marry a former nun** in Sydney. The pair has been granted various permissions by Head Office in the Vatican.

The ballyhoo over the astronauts **going to the moon has become stifling**. We are getting **headlines** that the astronauts are going first on a holiday, their children are being told of the risk, they are not worried about them being stranded, the space monkey Bonny will travel in a *primate transporter* crib.

MEDICAL TURMOIL AHEAD

In the year 2019, you can go to a GP anywhere in Australia and be pretty sure that the fee charged for the visit will be different from place to place, and from illness to illness. This is especially so if you go to a specialist.

But there is some uniformity, and if you get a rebate, it at least will be standardised.

But this was not always the case. In 1969, the system that now assures these benefits was just under development. All the interested parties had their hats in the ring, and were arguing why it was that each of them deserved to be paid more.

Doctors were in a fortunate position, when it came to raising the fees they charged. They did not have to **go before a tribunal and argue their case for an increase**. The nurses had to do this, and so too did chemists. But not the doctors. They could do this by a unilateral declaration.

This is what they did. They announced that their scale of fees would be increased. It had been just two years since their last increase, and now they were to be incremented by 10 to 22 per cent. This was at a time when GP's were losing their revered position in society, when they were reducing home visits, when they were putting formal time limits on visits, when they were putting on fees for after-hours visits, and when they were starting to push more patients towards higher expenditure on specialists and diagnostic testing.

Not surprisingly, the GPs attracted much criticism. The *SMH* led the attack. "It is this varied scale of rises - cynically and snobbishly attuned to what it thinks the market will bear - that gives their game away. And a sordid game it is too.... It is not enough to say that doctors, as professional men, have the right to charge what they like. Their fees are inescapable....Doctors have only themselves to blame if the Government decides in the future that their fees are too important to be decided by the doctors themselves".

The patient in the waiting room had plenty to say. It was all along the same line.

Letters, Catherine Smith. In 10 years of marriage we have required a plumber's visit **once** only. With five children, **the doctor's visits are endless**. In a recent severe measles bout in my family, the doctor paid 12 visits. Some were "multiple" visits (in 10 minutes he saw three patients!) But each was charged as a separate visit.

If it is pointed out to me that without modern medical care, my child may have died, I would answer that for this I thank the dedicated medical men and research chemists we have had in the past (and antibiotics). I do not thank the money-hungry sharks we have among us today.

Letters, W Jilliams. With all the controversy as to who should fill the role of Ned Kelly, Mick Jagger does not appear to be acceptable. Why not give that role to any of our suburban doctors? They lack nothing in the art of robbing the poor or the rich. Why not complete the cast and ask one of our suburban chemists to take the part of Ned's brother?

Letters, Joseph Lewis. A spokesman for the Australian Medical Association has said that one significant added burden has fallen on doctors employing trained nurses. These nurses recently received a pay increase of 20 per cent. One house call under the proposed new charges would account for the nurses' paltry pay rise, but it would appear that doctors want all their patients to pay it.

The spokesman for the doctors said that property rentals, rates and a host of other items had gone up, and the increases were justified.

A couple of writers came to the aid of the GPs.

Letters, A Turnbull. I am staggered by the attitude of some people who regard medical care as an automatic right. Today's physician is supposed to toil in response to these people's demands with little chance of reward, not necessarily monetary.

Last week a close personal friend astounded me by saying that I was no more than a technician and consequently did not deserve more material return for services rendered than the television repairman or the plumber.

To most people, the medical profession is still an honourable one, and I beseech these individuals to reconsider their values and place in perspective the benefits of good health compared to the maintenance of the luxuries in which we all indulge. Surely the gratitude of the nation should outweigh the criticisms of a fee increase imposed by an association that is attempting to enable its members to continue to practise, with humanity, in a materialistic society.

But the weight was very much against such GPs.

It was not only the GPs who came under criticism, though not so much for their fees. **Chemists, or pharmacists** as they are now known, were seen **by some** as pill pushers who were not worth they money they were paid. From this view-point, they received a prescription from a doctor, went to a bottle, and measured out the ingredient. Not much skill or training was needed, no specialised knowledge.

Letters, Barbara Allen, Lorna Cartwright, Pharmacy, University of Sydney. With all the consternation about an increase in dispensing fees, no one has considered the point that pharmacy is a profession, and pharmacists are equal in standing with doctors, dentists, lawyers, architects and scientists, requiring a university degree and professional experience before being allowed to practise.

We are entitled to be paid for our service as well as for goods. This service is not only "counting out tablets from one bottle to another," but also preparing extemporaneous medicines, which take considerably more than just five minutes, checking prescriptions for overdoses, for incompatibilities in formulation and also therapeutic incompatibilities. This can only be done by a person trained in pharmaceutics and pharmacology, to mention only two of the subjects studied.

The pharmacist today should be considered a drug consultant, the person of choice to whom a great number of the public still go for advice on drug medication and usage. Surely this training and service to the community entitle him to receive remuneration for his professional service.

Nurses too had their say for higher pay.

Letters, M Wilder. Medical fees are to rise again. Yet no power today appears to be able to give trained nurses a livable salary, much less a secure retirement. I am an experienced trained nurse and gave it all up three years ago because I considered the salary was an insult to my qualifications and experience.

Comment. Against this turmoil in medical costs, the Government was trying to bring down a system of universal medical insurance and hospital insurance. You can see, **from this small sample of matters unresolved**, that there was still a long way to go.

MOON STRUCK

On July 14, the News Services proclaimed that the weather looked good for a moon launch and they decided that the 17th would be the most likely date. The razza mataz and ballyhoo machines went into overdrive, right round the breathless world.

The three astronauts are ready to go, *Apollo 11* is sitting on its pad looking expectant, the Pope has sent an encouraging message. President Nixon had to cancel a dinner engagement with the astronauts because of fears that he might give them some disease. The Australian Prime Minister has agreed to send a message to the moon in a sealed capsule, and our Tracking Station at Parkes in NSW is reportedly moving sheep away from the Station as a security measure.

On July 15 it was confirmed that TV coverage of the moon walk would be shown locally, here in Australia. This would come from Parkes where a team of five Americans had been working for a month to set up a message relay system to the US. The team was led by John Hampton, actually an Australian, and a good friend of mine since University days. There were only two telescopes in the world that were capable of providing the services required, and Parkes was one of them.

On July 16, the weather was fine, a million citizens had assembled at Cape Kennedy. NASA had a guest list of 7,000 important people for the launching, and Australian marathon runner, Bill Emerton, had arrived after running from Texas. The astronauts will **not** be provided with suicide pills, and the maximum time they can spend on the moon is 36 hours.

On July 17th to 19th, blast off was successful, and followed by regular reports that the men were contented and "laconic". No troubles had been encountered and everything appeared to be on schedule. On Sunday 20th, the *Sun Herald* woke its readers with a huge headline saying "Big Day Tomorrow".

July 21st. After a 250,000 mile trip, and the passing of 102 hours, the three astronauts put foot on the moon. This generated much joy back in America, and indeed the rest of the world, and the astronauts were a bit chuffed as well. They wandered around for a while, planted a flag, got bored, and went back to their module and re-joined the space craft. In fact, it was a lot more exciting than it might seem from my few words above, and 600 million people watched it all excitedly on TV.

President Nixon captured the moment. "For one priceless moment in the history of mankind, all the people of the earth have become truly one: one in the pride of what you have done, and one in our prayers that you will return safely to earth."

The next few days, the trio retraced their steps. Finally, on July 25th, they parachuted down into the Pacific. They were picked up, sprayed with all sorts of protective substances, and then trundled off into 18 days of quarantine. The world heaved a sigh of relief, and as you know, lived happily ever after.

THE AFTERMATH

Politicians the world over sent congratulations, most of them implying they themselves were somehow partly responsible for the success. Americans, and their politicians, crowed incessantly, and reluctantly I have to admit, quite rightly too. Churches the world-over gave thanks, and everyone wanted to get into the act.

I will not attempt to describe all the activity. I will instead pick just one feature and leave you to imagine the rest. **Omega placed adverts in papers across the globe.** They showed pictures of the astronauts on the moon, a Swiss watch, and the following script.

THIS WATCH IS PRETTY SPECIAL

It's been strapped on the wrists of all US astronauts since 1965. It went on the first walk in space, and it made history by being the first watch worn by men on the moon.

It is Omega Speedmaster chronograph and it is the only watch flight-qualified by NASA for all manned space missions.

Yet even though this watch is pretty special, it is in fact **a standard-model Speedmaster. Unmodified. Straight off the production line.** Only the strap had to be specially made. NASA selected it because it was right for the job and could take the punishment.

The kind of punishment we're talking about makes other adventures seem like Sunday-school picnics. Imagine acceleration from zero to 24,600 miles an hour, powerful pressure changes; extreme temperatures and various other shocks which the unknown elements can dish out. All these things can seriously affect the accuracy of a watch. And when you are walking about in space you don't need that kind of problem. You don't get it with an Omega Speedmaster.

The Speedmaster is really tough. It had already been through hell and high water long before the NASA tests. It's just one of many specialised watches made by Omega that were developed for the rough-and-tumble of sports events. And this particular miniature time-computer has been in all kinds of cockpits apart from Apollo XI.

People tooling around Sebring or Monza or LeMans have found it invaluable to keep track of lap times. Lonely sailors push a button to record the time taken between a sextant sight and working out a "fix". Production engineers time machine output with it; TV producers time programme content; and so on in a variety of industries and professions.

The essential point is that Omega watches are made for people to whom time is critical. They are worn by professionals and they are tested to the ultimate limits of endurance.

What does it all mean to you? Just this. Everything which has been developed by Omega, regardless for which special purpose, finds its way into the everyday watch you buy if it has the name Omega.

Remember, all the watches in the famous Omega "Seamaster" range, a range of watches originally designed for nautical sports, have exactly the same unerring movement as those used by the Apollo astronauts. And each has the special features appropriate to the task for which it is intended.

If you visit your Omega jeweller, you will be shown watches that for precision, reliability, ruggedness features and style are the very best in the world. The Apollo astronauts proved them for you. Again.

Omega - first in space, first on the moon, first where it matters.

Comment. I am told that all of the 1,000's of mechanical components on the flight were equally impressive pieces of engineering. It was a fascinating and magnificent scientific and engineering feat. Congratulations to the Americans for being first, and to the Russians for being not far behind them.

If only the political world now was as smart as the scientific and engineering world was then.

ANOTHER KENNEDY DRAMA

In the USA, President John Kennedy was assassinated in 1963. His brother, Robert Kennedy, a candidate for the Presidency, was assassinated in 1968.

The third brother, Ted, during the moon-landing event, was coming home from a party, and drove his car off a bridge and into a largish pond. His passenger, a young girl, drowned in five feet of water. It took him about ten hours to report the incident to police.

There were many people who thought that there was more to the story. His political enemies were quick to cast doubt on his veracity. In the long run, he pleaded guilty to failing to report a traffic accident promptly, and was given a slap on the wrist.

All of this reflected on his political career, and he did not nominate for the 1972 elections as previously planned. In fact, he stayed in the dog-house until 1980, when he did run, but was defeated by Jimmy Carter in the Democratic Primaries.

THE SCORE KEEPS MOUNTING

In the last month, in Vietnam, eight Australian soldiers were killed and 69 badly wounded. About half of these were National Servicemen and the others were Regular Army.

THE EFFECTS OF PORNOGRAPHY

The clergyman below adds a sober element to the discussion on censorship.

Letters, Barry Bryant. In the controversy about censorship, it has often been declared that "censorship has never been proved to have an effect on anyone". The writers do not deny that there has been an increase in sexual aberration - in illegitimacy, in suicide, in pack rape - but they say there has never been any proof that what one reads or sees can have any bearings on such things.

Let me say that our entire education system is geared to the fact that **the quality of reading affects the quality of life and learning**.

The entire vast advertising industry of Australia is built on the foundation that if one sees something often enough, and convincingly enough, an attitude of acceptance will develop towards it. The entire commercial television and newspaper worlds are geared to the same belief.

What one sees and hears very strongly affects one's attitudes. Thus **the majority of us strongly support censorship**. We believes that pornography depraves and lowers the standards of people.

TRAGEDY IN VIETNAM

Letters, P Coleman. On behalf of the Australian Overseas Services Funds, may I extend our sympathies to the family of Miss Kathy Wayne who was shot dead while performing at a US base near

Da Nang recently.

We remember Miss Wayne for her bright personality when she toured with an official Australian Government party last year after volunteering her services to entertain troops.

Since AOSF starting sending concert parties in November 1965, we have had the protection and organisation of the Australian Army in Vietnam. Since then, more than 30 parties from the AOSF and the Army have been sent without incident.

We have frequently warned young performing artists against going independently to Vietnam, in view of the dangerous state of the country, but because the parties get the chance to work in the US Service Clubs, they take the risks, no doubt because of the emoluments.

Comment. This Letter is doubtless a genuine statement of grief. It also serves the purpose, I think, of diverting public blame from the AOSF, and maybe it also diverts it towards US organisations.

AUGUST NEWS ITEMS

Large eggs will be three cents a dozen cheaper from today....

This is a reminder that **prices of some goods (including eggs) were controlled by Governments**. Local gluts could come and go, but the price across the State stayed pegged by the authorities. **It was an offence to sell at anything but the proclaimed price.**

Two RAAF-balloonists set out from Perth to drift across the width of the nation. They hope to set a world distance record of 1,896 miles, and an endurance record of 96 hours....

The balloonists were forced down after 400 miles in 28 hours. They had already **broken the Australian record of 200 mile**s, but conditions were against them. They hope to make another attempt in under two weeks.

Conzinc Rio Tinto, an Australian Company, has a lease on land on the New Guinea island of **Bouganville**. **Villagers there refused to sell their land**, so it was forcefully acquired by NG Government decree....

CRA are intent on clearing many acres of land there. **The natives are resisting**, and yesterday a picket line was dispersed only by the use of tear gas and a baton charge by police. No one was injured, but it can be certain that this situation will fester.

Our various Governments are slowly becoming convinced of **the link between smoking tobacco products and the incidence of many diseases**, including cancer....

They are taking tentative steps towards putting a warning of the heath risks on the packets of cigarettes. The tobacco industry is responding by placing media ads that glamorise smokers. There are vast political forces at play here....

The tobacco industry around the world is extremely powerful, and controls many politicians. That industry is watching the Australian situation with much interest and a grim determination to resist every inch of the way.

Voters in NSW will be presented with a referendum question. "Do you favour the law being amended to permit hotels to trade between the hours of 12 noon and 6.30 pm?" The Premier said that the question was simple, and if, carried, the new legislation would allow hoteliers to decide not to trade if they thus chose. Fat chance....

He added that it would also require that direct entry to the hotel from the street not be allowed. Patrons would need to enter through a side door or through the residents' entrance. Fat chance....

I wonder who was behind this quaint, non-guaranteed puritanical provision?

Captain Robinson was in command of the RAN aircraft carrier *Melbourne* when it cut US destroyer *Frank E Evans* in two. Blame for the event clearly lies with the destroyer, but some smaller portion may attach to Robinson. To clarify this, he will face a Court-martial on two charges relating to the incident.

THOUGHTS ON POETRY

In all my writings, I have never published anything on poetry. Half the reason for that was because poetry did not generate any **news items** that I needed in my research. Doubtless, if I had looked elsewhere, I would have found lots of material. But I didn't.

The other half of the reason, I suppose, was that I have no understanding of poetry, and find it a silly waste of time. That is not a criticism of poetry, but rather a confession of my ignorance. And that stems, initially at least, from the absurd stuff that was forced on me at school under the name of poetry. Things like *The Lady of Shallot* and *Vitae Lampada.* Then later at university, in my moony period, the works of Byron and Shelly, who had no idea of straight talk. After that, poetry was for the dunces, and malcontents, the morbids, and the soppy do-gooders.

When I look at it now, I know that I was looking at the wrong type of poetry, and I always resolve to educate myself to its value and virtues. Over the last few years, I have found one good poet who talks a bit in my own language and about things that matter a bit to me.

That poet is Les A Murray. He is about my age, an Australian born at Nabiac, not too far away, and who has been writing for 40 years, and who has been proclaimed by the National Trust of Australia as one of this nation's 100 National Treasures.

When I saw this Letter below from him in the *SMH*, I just had to make up for my past neglect, and publish it no matter what its content was. So, here it is.

Letters, Les A Murray. I was dismayed to read last weekend that 10 highly qualified **scientists** fear they will be forced to leave Australia because of an "appalling" lack of jobs for them and many of their fellows.

If **scientists** are so hard done by, then **the outlook for poets** must be grim indeed.

Solidarity with a deprived and frustrated scientific community may be a new idea for some of us, in this country at any rate, but I am sure we will find some way to welcome them into the club. Mental agility is part of a poet's stock-in-trade, after all. It is all rather depressing, though.

I was going to suggest to our Government that it consider following the example of Eire in making all income earned from works of cultural and artistic merit tax-free, but the sad plight of Australia's scientists has shamed me out of that proposal. Perhaps Ireland, with its booming economy, is ready for social changes of this sort, but clearly we are not.

I would say to my fellow poets: be of good heart and keep reading the Press. Vacancies for poets will start appearing some day, and that will be better than any old Irish tax dodge. Somewhere between physicists and psychologists is the general area to watch.

Comment. It's too wafty for me, and I doubt if it effected any policy changes. Still, as I indicated above, the world of poets and poetry is foreign to me. So how would I know?

COMPULSORY LAND ACQUISITION

In this segment, I will talk about **the resumption of land** by various Authorities. I will start with New Guinea, and gradually turn to mainland Australia.

In my News Items for this month, I talked about the problems on Bouganville. This Letter below was written before the riot I mentioned in those Items.

Letters, University of New England Interests (11 persons). The compulsory resumption-acquisition of land for the sake of "progress" is always questionable.

What is happening in Bougainville - the compulsory, police-enforced acquisition of land for Conzinc Riotinto's copper project - is an extension of the paternalistic techniques being used by "liberal" white Australia against its long-suffering, long-humiliated Aborigines.

Few Australians of this generation are not sickened by the history of European colonisation and, in particular, by the arbitrary dispossession of the land of the Australian Aborigines.

One hoped that this would not be repeated in our time. An idle hope! Today the natives of the Amazon are being dispossessed of their lands with the added refinements of the machine-gun and the aeroplane. And, nearer at home, the Bougainville Islanders are being forced to give up their land by "processes of law" - a law imposed on these people from the outside.

The sale of their heritage in land will, no doubt, be

followed by a flood of salesmen seeking quick profits in washing machines, cars, liquor, even drugs, and other unnecessary trappings of our much-vaunted "civilisation." Almost inevitably those islanders who survive action by the mainland New Guinea police in execution of the Administration's policy will, in a few years, form a further addition to the dispossessed fringe-dwellers of European-style towns.

It is claimed by the Administration of Papua-New Guinea - agents in this matter to the Australian Government - that the alienation of native lands is for the "betterment of the Territory." How can anyone argue in justification of the taking of a community's land and the minerals under it - both owned in natural right by the traditional occupiers of the land? And, as for benefits, who else but Conzinc Riotinto will gain in any substantial degree from an agreement entered into by the Australian Government, which now finds that its commitments to this overseas-owned company are in conflict with the rights of the people of one of its United Nations Trust territories?

Comment. The compulsory acquisition of land is not new. I suppose it started for Australia when the white man started taking land from the black man. And it has always happened when the rich and powerful, or genuine benefactors, wanted to build structures in areas where other people had congregated. Some of it was truly for the public good, and some of it was not.

On Bouganville, the natives, who are being bought out, will suffer. On the other hand, the whole nation is backward and badly needs to develop whatever resources it can. Using the copper deposits look an easy way to do this. Can a relatively small number of people deny economic benefits to an entire nation? In Australia, should a few home-owners stop the building of a highway, or a railway, or an airport.

The fight in Bouganville is a prelude to the famous and familiar battle in the classic Australian film *The Castle*. But it was happening not only in remote islands, but also in the innermost parts of our big cities and towns.

OTHER NEFARIOUS PRACTICES.

There are other related practices that writers are complaining about. Many of them **had properties resumed** to have roads or railways put through their areas of living. Take for example, Tom Brooks below.

Letters, T Brooks, near Gosford. I got a compulsory resumption order a month ago, and my 25 acres will be resumed for a planned town bi-pass that will be started in 1975. The offer is based on 1969 prices.

I do not want to move, but know I will have to. That is, move in 1975. But if I move then, I will need to find new premises. At 1975 prices. But the Government will only give me 1969 prices.

I will be well out of pocket. In any case, I will have to move further out, away from my market. I have ruin staring me in the face.

Then there is another farmer from Singleton with a variation on this.

Letters, A Meeks. I had a similar situation to

Mr Brooks. But after eight months, the plan has changed and the offer to me was withdrawn before I could settle, but after I had committed to a new property. So now I have **two** properties. But I can hardly afford **one**. What a mess.

Many endings will not be as happy for the resistance as it was in *The Castle* movie.

FURTHER ARGUMENTS ABOUT BOUGANVILLE

Were the locals being ripped off by the white man? Was the price offered a fair one, and would the natives change their minds if the price was raised? Should CRA go away, and let the natives live on the way they had for centuries? Would they be better off or worse off if this happened?

There were plenty of questions, and no shortage of writers who offered advice.

The Editor of the *SMH* pointed out that nothing is more important to the indigenous people of Bouganville than land. Apart from providing for the economic necessities, it has **immense spiritual and spiritual significance** as well. He pointed out that the Bouganvillians had no affection for the other people on New Guinea, and in fact would prefer to secede from the rest of the country. On top of that, the sales of land would be made to **Europeans**, and that was for them a compelling argument against sales.

He concludes that "arguments that the sales will benefit the whole of the country are anything but persuasive in this parochial atmosphere."

However, as it inevitably happens, whenever you think you have a good handle on an argument, someone else pops up with another side to it all.

Letters, D Vertigan. There is one matter which may not be clear in the reports I have seen concerning the land being acquired from one group. As I recall, **the Rorovana people have only been in the area since late last century.** They, and the occupants of two other nearby villages, came from the British Solomon Islands after tribal quarrels, and are a different people from others in that portion of Bougainville. That they had not been there long they admitted freely at the time I knew them, and, in 1932, they took me to see an old woman who came in the first canoes from the British Solomon Islands.

Their ownership of land is therefore quite recent, probably based on settlement or gift from other people in the area. While their title may be good, it cannot be considered to have the same symbolical and spiritual quality which is attached to land which has been in people's possession from time immemorial as is the general rule in New Guinea and the islands.

PRE-SCHOOL EDUCATION

Kindergartens in 1969 were not thick on the ground. There might have been one in the richer city suburbs, and perhaps one in every regional city. But they were for an elite, and probably only for half a day, and mainly for four-year-olds to give them a head start on formal school education. There was no concept that working mothers could use them.

But the times were starting to change.

Letters, FOUR MOTHERS. Congratulations on your editorial bringing to light the desperate plight of pre-school education in NSW.

The State Government is the biggest landlord in this area. The facilities provided for children of all ages, especially of pre-school age, are hopelessly inadequate, and practically non-existent.

If the Government thinks there is no issue, it is sadly mistaken. We are determined to make an issue of it. We consider our children's welfare of vital importance. What are our local members doing to support us? Absolutely nothing! Beware! We militant mothers are in a fighting mood!

Comment. The argument among women against the idea of hired help to look after children was a worry that children, without the constant attendance of a clucking mother, would not grow up as a rounded person, or the like. Some mothers, with a capital M, were adamant that if children came home to an empty house, or if the mother was not keeping the household in order, then the children would turn to delinquency, or mischief, or - a new threat - drugs.

But these were early years. As you know, millions of women have since joined the workforce, thousands of kindies of all types have been funded by the Government, and more thousands of women are employed looking after hordes of children from every imaginable class.

Further note. Let me add that, from where I sit, it seems that the possessive mothers need not have worried. Children, for the most part enjoy the kinder, and do equally as well as their more closeted elders.

POINTS FOR DUEL CITIZENS

I know you have been waiting for news about duelling, and indeed I have been anxious because so far I have given you none. Now, I am happy to say, a drib has come through, and while it is just an apologia for duelling, it will assure you that the fine sport of duelling is still well and thriving. **I remind you that duelling is not fencing.** It is fair dinkum duelling, and cuts and shootings are probable.

Letters, H Schultze. Excuse my temerity in adding some observations to your Weekend Magazine article, "Where a scar is a badge of manhood". To have taken dueling out of its social context is, of course, unbalanced.

One may assume that every sport has its roots in a mystery tradition of the heroic, be it football or cricket. It may seem strange and unfair to a German watching cricket, where **one single man is opposed by the combined skill of 11 men of his opposing team**, and he may be tempted to make a similar observation to that your Cecil Henderson did.

There are many of us who have undergone unscathed the ordeal of fencing on the Paukboden, because it was undertaken in the satisfaction of honour rather than the outward marking of face. No doubt many have facial scars to be fashionable, or to follow in the steps of their "Alte Herrn", or some even to gain a place in society because of their lack of antecedents. Yet the purpose of dueling clubs was to teach the single student the responsibility of each and every word he utters and the responsibility of each and every action he does. Whatever he does or utters must be worth his life or else let him keep his peace.

Every student, as a prospective leader in his society, must be aware that freedom of speech in his particular calling must be supported by that sense of social responsibility and ultimately by his own life. Many of us have experienced the difficulties of later life when honour becomes equated with worldly success, but have refused to be drawn into the vortex of aspirations of more and greater wealth and social standing.

After all, is this not one of the principles of our Christian faith?

Comment. The Letter makes a few references that I will not track down, and it expresses sentiments that I hope I subscribe to. In any case, I commend it to you, and hope you find much peace in your life through the ancient sport of duelling.

DRIVE-INS FOR CLUBS

Government say that drive-ins would not be allowed for clubs. They say you can get a drink there, and bring your family there to eat, but not to stock up on grog that you can then take home to drink. To do that would be outside the purpose of setting up clubs in the first place.

Comment. Probably fair enough.

SEPTEMBER NEWS ITEMS

A study done in the Queensland city of Townsville found that **country children had lower IQs than city children**. They were also more introverted and more anxious.

A physicist at Sydney University, Professor McCusker, has found and photographed the **evidence of quark**s, the so-called building blocks of nature....

I and many of my generation will have been **brought up to believe that "the atom is the smallest particle of matter"**. If McCusker is correct, we will have to **re-write the text books**....

As you know, he was spot on.

400 people turned up at Canberra Railway Station with their pockets full of money. Rumours had been started in local pubs, and spread across the nation in a week, that **brand new WWII Jeeps could be bought there for $30 plus rail cost.** The story was that Canberra was the only place that the right-hand-drive vehicles could be registered....

But there was no one there selling at 10 a.m. There was no sign of Jeeps. In fact, it was a big hoax. **People from as far away as Perth had to go home by train.**

Batteries have been found in a number of saddles after horse race meetings about Sydney. **Four men have been disqualified.** One such person told the Committee "I don't care what you do to me, but **this game is crook and will be for ever**"....

At that time, many people agreed with him.

For cricket followers. It is reported that an Australian girl from Melbourne **will marry Gary Sobers** soon. Let us hope she has more success in bringing him to heel than our own cricketers ever did....

Such marriages between **a black man and a white woman were uncommon at the time**.

Lang Hancock, the Australian mining magnate and millionaire, is another person who **wants to use nuclear power to make his business easier**. He wants to bore holes 800 miles deep at the iron ore mine at Wittenoom in Western Australia....

Then, with **one big bang,** he wants to **set off nuclear explosions** that will completely displace enormous tonnages of iron ore, that he can them scoop up and export....

The odds are that he won't get Government approval.

NSW is likely to allow adult status at the age of 18. That means young people will be able to enter into **contracts and wills, probably serve on juries,** and possibly vote. Though voting changes would mean that **all** the States would have to co-operate. Most unlikely....

It could mean that youths receive **adult rates of pay**. Also, it may become possible for them **to play poker machines, and buy lottery tickets....**

"After all, centuries ago youths attained adulthood at 14."

OUR STANDARD ON RADIO

The writer below has an interesting idea. He talks about some strange device called FM radio.

Letters, H Vallentine. Sydney's seven radio stations provide a total of 126 hours of broadcasting a week between 6am and midnight. Only seven per cent of this, on the average, is good music, and almost all of that is provided by the ABC.

For seven of the 14 hours to 8pm there is no such music and little else of quality, apart from the ABC's service broadcasts.

Our real need is a third program, preferably on FM (frequency modulation) such as most other cities of any size in the Western World enjoy, because the general level of radio and TV fare available here is little short of disgraceful.

Yet we are being pressured to finance colour television, which could cost the country $1,000 million dollars in sets alone, without bringing any prospect of improved quality of fare.

Our large cities might benefit from a Radio and TV Consumers' society which could exert pressure on the ABC, the commercial stations and their sponsors, and on the Federal Government. Its aim could be to press for FM and also to press for more time to be given to quality broadcasts, co-ordinated so that something of value is available somewhere on the air throughout the day.

Comment. I do not fully understand what he is talking about. It seems to me that changing the method of delivery will not change the actual content. Bad programmes will still be bad programmes.

Still, probably he knows better than I do. And, anyway, probably no one will heed him, and this FM radio stuff will never happen.

SMOKING AND CANCER

The link between smoking tobacco products and cancer, and other pulmonary disease, was slowly getting more obvious. But there was opposition from the tobacco companies and from smokers themselves. Always they raised the cry "my granddad smoked all his life, and it never hurt him".

The Letter below gives an indication of where the argument was in 1969. Nothing was quite clear, and any new findings were met by masses of denials by the tobacco companies.

Letters, (Dr) O Briscoe. It is disappointing to see yet another complaint attributed to the tobacco industry, that the evidence associating tobacco with health hazards has been exaggerated, being "only statistical."

Since many widely accepted contemporary medical beliefs are supported by similar evidence, perhaps they too are unsound? Thus, for example, many people think that the tubercle bacillus, the poliomyelitis virus, and insufficiency of dietary Vitamin C have causal relationships to pulmonary TB, poliomyelitis and scurvy respectively.

Although not everyone exposed to these hazards develops the clinical disease, the incidence in those exposed is statistically highly significant.

It is pertinent that in days gone by, experienced physicians are said to have refused to believe that a dietary factor could be the cause of scurvy because they saw some undernourished patients who did not develop the disease.

The link between smoking and ill-health is statistically incontrovertible; we may lack for some time the technical knowledge to demonstrate the precise physio-chemical or pharmacological mechanisms involved but this really does not invalidate the statistical correlation. What use individuals make of the warnings they receive is their own affair, but to question the use of warnings and advertising control seems a pity.

OZ PRONUNCIATION

Every few years, someone sets the Letters Columns ablaze with a criticism of the way that our newsreaders and others mess up the English language. Here is a starter.

Letters, J Shayler. Although the speech of Australians has shown a marked improvement over the past 30 years, an appalling number of words still are mispronounced, often by people who ought to know better.

Foremost among these is secretary, pronounced by most of our politicians and even by the ABC's speakers and news commentators as *seckatry*.

The next most frequent solecism is temporary, which has become *tempory*: related to this word is the much-abused contemporary, and this has suffered a like fate. We hear about somebody's *perogative*, and a number of the voices which answer the telephone weather service announce that the forecast is issued by the Bureau of *Meteology.*

Particularly has been contracted to *particuly* - but the list of badly enunciated words is a long one.

CONVICTIONS

Drink-driving laws across the nation were changing all the time. But every State recognised that the more people drank the more smashes they had. And that more lives were lost and more injuries were suffered.

So, despite the disruption caused by the ever-changing traffic rules, the States were all making headway **under the law** in punishing motorists who drank and drove.

In NSW, for example, **doctors were called to the scene of an accident** only if the police were satisfied that a driver was under the influence. **In other States, no doctor was every involved,** and tests were applied to the driver on the spot, and then a decision was made. If, for example, the driver staggered or could not tip-toe a straight line, he was gone. I will summarise by saying that charges were not as yet based on firm incontrovertible evidence.

When such matters came to Court, however, in most cases the Judges and Magistrates were on a chummy basis with the police, and so almost all cases went through accepting the judgement of the constables involved.

But some magistrates had their own views. One was issuing penalties **well in excess of those set down by law.** On the other hand, another was increasingly **challenging**

the police, and finding the defendant not guilty. He even went so far as to reverse some guilty decisions made in other Courts. This could not go on. Imagine the loss of revenue if every driver who said he was innocent was given his fine back. So the authorities were putting pressure on the Magistrate to see **the error of his ways.**

But the public was having its say as well. You can well imagine that red-necks were much in support of the reversed decisions. And also that there were many others who took the opposite approach that said the rules were there to stop the road carnage, and to pervert them in the Courts of law was wrong. If need be, toughen up the rules, but do not let their purpose be frustrated. Anyway, back to public opinion.

Letters, Solicitor. The Governor's annulment of convictions imposed by a magistrate is, in my view, a highly improper exercise of political interference by the Minister in the administration of justice.

How can the Minister say that "the motorists concerned had been wrongly convicted" when they all failed to attend court to answer the traffic charges listed for hearing? Moreover, if a penalty is deemed too severe, there is a Court of Appeal to apply to.

Furthermore, statistics show that the magistrate's tough penalties on certain motorists have materially reduced the road toll in the Wollongong area.

The worst feature of the Minister's action is that political interference in the administration of justice in the police courts is wrong in principle, and is likely to undermine the discipline of, and respect for, these admirable Courts and the excellent work they perform.

Letters, W Robinson. Your recent Letter regarding annulment of convictions is either a pathetic illustration of a solicitor jumping to conclusions or a critic voicing his opinion on a matter of which he is completely ignorant.

As a motorist who has had a conviction annulled, I have reason to know that the Government only acts where there is fault on the part of the administration, or the conviction, on its face, is bad in law, e.g. imposes a fine in excess of that permitted for the offence.

In my case, a magistrate convicted me despite the fact that no summons had been served on me. Obviously I was not present in court for the proceedings. As I was neither the driver nor owner of the car referred to in the summons, nor had I ever heard of it, I would most certainly have defended the matter had I been give the opportunity.

Even "Solicitor" will agree that one can only appeal if the conviction comes to notice in time to do so, and had mine not been annulled, I would have had no redress at all. I am aware of many other examples where defects have come to notice after conviction.

Comment. Of course, there were lots of others who had their say. In fact as the years rolled on, and as the rules got tougher and tougher, this was one of the really persistent

Letters topics that was guaranteed to split the community of Letter-writers every time there was another change.

PENNIES FROM GOVERNMENT

As readers look **back** towards 1969, it is easy to think that the various Governments and Councils have always been able to find new ways to extract heaps of money from ordinary citizens, or to put more regulations and rules on them.

For example, as we have seen, the laws on drink driving have toughened up. But in lots of other areas as well. Building codes are stricter, no smoking is allowed in many areas, we now pay GST, even on small purchases from overseas. Packaging laws are now on all the boxes we buy, health and safety regulations make all workers look alike, TV operates under a strict code restricting smut, and filth and violence.

That is not to say that all these changes are bad for us. It is simply saying that our world is getting more civilised, and **the price of that civilisation is more regulations**, and so more rules are enforced, and more money needs to be collected to pay for them.

But wait a minute. It is not a one way street. Sometimes we get something important back.

Let me give you two examples from 1969.

Letters, Irene Lewis, NSW Women Justices' Association. It is interesting to read of the large, increased amount collected by the State Government over the last 12 months for stamp and death duties.

The increase in **the death duties** collected would be due to a large extent to increased valuations of real estate. My association has for some time made representations to the Premier to raise the statutory exemption of $20,000 on small estates where the estate is left to the widow, widower and children under the age of 21 years, because, due to rising valuations, the present exemption is out of date.

In view of the extent of home ownership (about 75 per cent to 80 per cent) elderly people in particular could suffer considerable hardship to find quite a substantial amount for death duty levied on the matrimonial home in the event of the death of either the husband or the wife.

Comment.   Glory be.   Death duties have not been increased.   There are no problems with limits changing. **In fact, death duties have been abolished. Completely.** What a great boon to families that have worked hard to accumulate assets, and faced the loss of large percentages them through death duties.

The second example.

Letters, E Young. A lot is said on high taxation of the middle-income group, but shareholders, small or great, are double-taxed. They own the companies they are in. The company earns profits and the Federal Government takes 42$1/2$ per cent of it in tax.

What is received as dividend is taxed again as part of the shareholder's income. If he has a high income he may be taxed at 50 per cent! But what of the widows and small holders? There are many with dividend incomes of less than $1,000 a year.

Put it to your Federal member.

Comment. As the above argument explains, double taxation had been vexatious for years. But since those bad old days, **a new system of imputation credits has been introduced**, and that means that most people get most of **their double taxation back from the Taxation Department**. Of course, it is fair and reasonable that they should. But not everyone cares all the time about those virtues.

SAVE OUR ROOS - MAYBE

We live in a country that has unique animals, and most people want to see it kept that way. We also live in a nation that earns a lot of its bread and butter from agricultural pursuits. In the happiest of worlds, we could keep our animals and our prosperity.

But we can't do this. Sometimes, the two aspirations must clash. In this case, our farmers and our kangaroos have different ideas about what our happiest world should be like.

The roos see a field of wheat shoots and want to chew and romp on it. This incidentally destroys it for the season. The farmers just want to be left alone. If they had **set-and-forge**t wheat crops, that would be their idea of happiness. But the damn roos are always there threatening their livelihood.

So, one side or other, usually the farmers, get a gun and shoot away. But the other side, roo lovers, have something to say about this.

Letters, B Green. In the name of decency, what can be done to stop this indiscriminate slaughter of these defenceless creatures? Granted that at times we must exercise some control over kangaroo populations, but surely the bloodbath being indulged in by professional shooters must trouble the conscience of even the most hardened and unfeeling in the community.

Butchery on the scale described in this article (119 kills in one night, an estimated 190,000 in eight years, by one man) can have but one result - extermination of most species of this unfortunate animal. And there are believed to be 1,600 shooters active in Queensland alone!

Is not this an appalling situation and one crying for far more stringent action by Commonwealth and State Governments?

Have we not learned the bitter lessons of the past when, for example, **the koala bear was only just saved from extinction in Queensland**? Only eleventh-hour Government action, demanded by a public aroused almost too late by the barbarity of those engaged in the profitable export of thousands upon thousands of skins, prevented the annihilation of koalas in that State.

The butcher who described his experiences to Mr Hudson speaks very matter of factly about his trade, and is totally absorbed in making as much money as he can from this sordid business in as short a time as possible. If this is the attitude of all those others who profit by such devastation of our wildlife resources, the future presents a very bleak picture indeed.

Those who love this country and the unique fauna that has developed here have warned may times of the consequences of wanton destruction. Must their protests continue to be as "voices crying in the wilderness"?

Even their ankle-biters have something to add.

Letters, Grant Patterson (aged 8). I love our Australian animals. And I think it is cruel the way they are killed. If every girl and boy shouted out loudly, "STOP killing little animals," perhaps these men might hear them.

If they keep killing them, there won't be any left.

But it all comes back to the same argument. Where do you draw the line between the roos and the farmers? You can try to exterminate completely one class or the other, but that is too drastic. **As for the roos**, you can license professional shooters to help with this, but that is scratching the surface. You can put in measures to poison them, but they keep coming back at some time down the track. You can fence your crops, but roos seem to like defying fences.

To me, all I can do is shrug my shoulders, as I do **every time this problem comes to the fore.** Keep a balance, realise that there are competing demands, and avoid extreme solutions. That is all I can offer.

But I bet there are a lot or readers, farmers or roos, who think quite differently.

FURTHER NEWS ON FM RADIO

Letters, Ray Allsop. The PMG said in Parliament on June 6, 1968: "FM has certain merits, including lower noise levels and higher fidelity of sound. While these characteristics are real **they are not**, in the opinion of this Government, **sufficiently significant to justify the introduction of a new service.** They would be valued, of course, by a limited section of the community, such as music lovers... but today's radio programs, which include a lot of pop music, open-line programs and so on, would not make good use of the qualities of FM even if it were introduced."

But it points out that it has been active in promoting stereo sound broadcasts.

Letters, Ray Allsop. In August, the ABC presented a program of stereophonic music via 2BL and 2FC. Listeners required two receivers, one tuned to BL the other to FC, to hear the sound in audio perspective, the two transmitters and two receivers representing the two human ears in extension.

Comment. It's all happening.

OCTOBER NEWS ITEMS

October 2nd. Nickel was discovered in remote Windana in Western Australia. A company called **Poseidon Nickel** was listed all this year on the Australian Stock Exchanges. In September, the normally-idle **shares showed some speculative life, but as** the drilling reports came in, the shares jumped from $5 to $12....

A few other nickel-related shares showed a small rise in sympathy. **Who knows? Maybe the whole market will get a bit of a fillip.**

Our Minister for **National Development is certain** that our first nuclear power station **will be in operation in seven years time**. The most likely location will be on the NSW coastal town of Jervis Bay. He says that it will be fuelled by our own "indigenous" uranium....

It could be that he was correct in his forecast, and that it is just his timing that is a bit out.

In NSW, **steam trains** have almost disappeared. The **last two** still running will make their **last trip on October 10th.**

Australia is heading for Federal elections soon. The Labour Party has been **out of office since 1950**, and the leadership of Gough Whitlam is raising hopes that it **might stand a chance this time round....**

A big worry for that Party is that some Catholic voters have formed a separate Party, called **the Democratic Labor Party**. This DLP, which deplores the big influence that the Communists have on the Labour Party,

could split the vote, and give control back to the sitting Liberals again.

Oct 6th. *HMAS Melbourne*, **the flagship of our national fleet**, has been in dry dock at Cockatoo Island since it crashed with the American destroyer *Frank E Evans*....

Although all repairs have been completed, **it had been held in the dock for four weeks** by the NSW Labour Council over a wages dispute for the Unions involved in its repairs. The Council had just voted to expand its ban on the movement of the ship....

The Navy **has had enough, and** will move the vessel out next Monday. If it then seeks further repairs at another dry dock, **the unionists there will not work on it until the pay dispute is settled....**

Who did run the country? Does anyone run it now?

October 9th. Poseidon shares are now priced at $23.

Federal elections will be held in a few weeks. The current Prime Minister, **John Gorton**, says that he is 3 to 1 on to win. **Most commentators agree that he will be lucky to break square....**

Opposition Leader, **Gough Whitlam, thinks he will gain 24 seats**, and thus have an easy win....

A Gallop Poll reported that **Gorton's support over the last three months has fallen** from 64 to 44....

I remind you that if Labor wins, it will be **its first victory in almost 20 years.**

A MONTH OF TRIVIA

In most Chapters of this book, I have dealt with one or two big issues, and then gone onto smaller stuff.

Not so this Chapter. I intend to deal with smaller matters all the way. This will help to give you a view of life in the suburbs and towns, and where the action is for the men and women in the street. Whatever are they talking about?

SAVE THE MONSTER

Letters, V Gilling. In the "Herald" of September 13 there was an article on the proposed method for "cornering" the Loch Ness monster.

Surely, animal-lovers throughout the world must feel appalled to read that 40 men from the British film industry intend to use "terrifying noises," such as sonic booms, etc., for this purpose.

Why does the British RSPCA not prevent such wanton cruelty to an unfortunate and seemingly harmless creature, if such a creature truly exists?

One wonders if the poor animal when "cornered" will attack its tormentors and, as in many instances, when animals have suffered torture and teasing, will be "done away with."

Comment. I have it on good authority that the monster simply outwitted its tormentors. On the days of the sonic booms, it simply stayed out of sight, and waited for all the bally-hoo to go away. After that, it just went on with its normal life, coming up for air when and if it wanted to.

MORE MIGRANTS NEEDED?

Australia's motto at the moment was "Populate or Perish". The Government thought that we had such a small population that we could not defend ourselves, and that if we bred copiously we could then avoid being over-run. Also, to boost our numbers, it was encouraging more than 150,000 migrants a year to come here so that we could count them.

The Feds said that the influx of migrants helped the nation because they purchased more goods, and because many of them brought with them some skills that this nation needed. I can remember that for years we needed pastry cooks, and they were at the top of the list.

Despite the dubious reasoning, this policy prevailed in 1969, and continues to do so right up to the present time. But at least one person thought this was a bad thing.

Letters, M Thompson. Denis Warner's article on migration policy hinged on a popular idea which I believe should not go unquestioned.

He states: "... our need for people is great." Is this really true? The Scandinavian countries have maintained a high standard of living with smaller populations than ours. Many of the big problems in the world - pollution of the environment, food shortages, unemployment - are due to large populations. I don't believe Australia will stagnate if we do not gain migrants.

I am not suggesting we should close our borders, but I do believe we should stop actively seeking migrants both in Europe and Asia.

Comment. The arguments that Mr Thompson and others put was that we had housing shortages. These migrants made them worse. Also, we had limited jobs. These migrants took them. We had limited resources. Guess who took them.

Fifty years later, with an annual net migrant intake of 220,000, maybe these latter arguments are being heeded. And maybe not.

WHAT A MESSY LOT

There is no doubt that Australians in 1969 were careless with their wrappings. For example, for decades, shopkeepers near the beaches had complained that patrons came into their fish-and-chips shop, bought a piece of fish and a few chips, then ate them on the boulevards and dropped the newspaper wrapping in the gutter. There have also been constant complaints against similar villains who stick their chewing gum everywhere, and even from theatre owners who despair over people dropping half-eaten ice cream cones on the floor.

You can see it is a serious matter. But one writer offers a solution.

Letters, Faith Fogarty. I wish to express my hearty support for the new Lord Mayor's professed intention to squash Sydney's litterbugs.

Lately I have been studying the behaviour of these creatures, and have noticed particularly that they, especially the young ones, stroll along the streets shedding ice-cream wrappers and orange peelings without so much as a furtive glance around to see if anyone is observing them.

This leads me to believe that most litterbugs are simply unconscious of their actions. So the obvious first step in an anti-litter campaign would be to make these people aware that their disposal habits are definitely offensive. Merely dotting the footpaths with bilious green rubbish bins in the hope of attracting the eyes of potential litterbugs has proved insufficient.

As a possible anti-litter program I suggest that the City Council contract commercial film agencies to make short films or animated cartoons vividly illustrating the litter problem and that these films be supplied to movie theatres and TV stations for repeated showings so no one escapes the message.

The campaign must be actively taken up by primary and secondary schools to catch young people while they are still in an impressionable stage of development.

Service stations, too, could be encouraged to dispense litterbags for cars.

Another writer offers a harsher solution.

Letters, Marie Earl. At 8.30 on a Saturday morning in Archer Street, Chatswood, a young man in a car threw a complete newspaper out the window. There is just one way of curing such litterbugs: by heavy fines. Mrs Fogarty's suggestion of educational films for children would need to be supplemented by **penalties** for young offenders such as gathering up the litter outside their local milk bar or picture theatre.

For the adult community, how about numerous eye-catching posters on which "$100 fine" looms large and clear as well as reminders on radio and TV? This could be followed by the odd, but regular, prosecution of offenders by the police, well publicised by the Press. Finally it's for the parents to restrain themselves and teach their children that littering is as unacceptable in a civilised society as the old-time custom of throwing the bedroom slops out the window.

Comment. Where do you draw the line? Suppose a person drops a chewing gum wrapper? Would he be fined? Would the police be better employed hounding real criminals?

Second comment. I agree with the above sentiments. Oz was a messy place and needed some jolt that would wake it up. Though I think that a better solution would be to provide lots more bins, bilious green or not.

In 1969, there were virtually no bins in public places. People could walk through a city suburb for miles and not find a bin. One motorist drove from Sydney GPO to Newcastle GPO, right through the suburbs, because there were no highways then, and did not see a single bin on his left-hand-side.

Further comment. Fifty years later, in fact there are a lot more bins, and the streets are much cleaner. Young people have come to the party in making this happen, and indeed are generally quite fastidious.

RECRUITMENT OF ASIAN NURSES

All State Governments are bemoaning the fact that they can't recruit nurses. Instead of doing the obvious of asking why not and fixing the problems, some are going to the Philippines and Japan and recruiting nurses there. These poor bewildered girls, who do not speak a word on English, are put into wards immediately, and are left to cry the nights away.

Letters, Robin Ryan, NSW Association for Immigration Reform. Recent letters to the "Herald" concerning a scheme to recruit trainee nurses in Asia reflect a widespread and most understandable wish that Australian nurses shall not be hampered in their efforts for better pay and working conditions.

The fact is that the admission of nurses from countries which can spare them could make the working days (and nights) of an Australian nurse in an understaffed hospital less onerous than they are now. Several officers of the NSW Association for Immigration Reform are university teachers who have found their loads somewhat lightened when vacancies were eventually filled by valued Asian colleagues.

The great need is to ensure that any intake of nurses, whether visiting trainees or immigrants, shall be strictly regulated, so that pressure to maintain and improve the rewards of nursing will continue. No one will lose if the entry of Asians eases specific labour shortages, but it would be a tragic mistake for hospitals or other institutions to become dependent on services rendered by members of ethnic minorities. There seems to be no risk whatever of such a situation arising.

Letters, G Say. What a generous people we Australians are! When professional conditions deteriorate to such a degree that few intelligent Australian girls, no matter how humanitarian they are, attempt a nursing career, the White Australia barrier is removed. Now Malaysian girls are welcomed for training.

When are the youth from Asian nations going to be greeted, not just as short-term students and nursing labour, but as fellow human beings with equal rights?

When will they be given the opportunity of promotion to responsible positions instead of being bundled off back home after basic training?

No wonder the "Herald" is so insistent on extensive defence requirements. This treatment of Asians as inferiors, which is, at its best, paternalistic, will ensure that at some future time we will need every defence we can muster.

Letter, Ray Ford. G Say's Letter strayed from the point. She said that it was only **after** conditions for our nurses got so bad that Asians have been sought. She should have, **but did not**, stress that what we should have done was **improve conditions for Australian nurses**.

Give the local girls a decent wage, and good working conditions, and they will flock to the job. They have big hearts, and broad shoulders, and will be delighted to show that.

But one other improvement is necessary. Get rid of the iron-fisted matrons and senior sisters who bring their terror to young nurses. You do not have to be a martinet to get the best out of young people. Just good wages and conditions, and treat them as if they are valuable workers and decent adults.

ORGANISING A WAR

When this nation goes to war, a lot of effort is involved. Wars don't grow on trees, and thousands of people are employed to make sure that every one is a success. Most of them are sensible persons who do their best and would be the first to acknowledge that despite this, mistakes will happen and all that they can do about them is fix them, and make sure that they do not happen again.

Such was the case in this unfortunate matter below.

Letters, Terence Cutcliffe. I became 20 years old last February. By a notice from the Registrar of National Service, I was informed that I had been selected for service. I do not know if my birth date was drawn in the ballot or not. If the Government conducts an honest ballot why are not the birth dates of young men selected for service published?

Why does the Government expect a second son of one family to do two years' army training **when one son has already died** while undergoing National Service training in Vietnam? My brother, a National Serviceman, was killed in Vietnam in August 1967.

Understandably, to save distress to my family and parents, I do not wish to undergo National Service "training." The Government offers me two years in prison if I refuse - a very humane alternative from a Government which obviously considers statistics in preference to families.

As a minor, I do not have the right to record a vote of protest against the Government.

Comment. Some weeks later, regulations were changed so that the brothers of a boy killed in National Service would not be called up.

FREE BUSES FOR KIDS

In NSW, and several other States, authorities were aware of the increasing costs imposed in attending school. One of these was the high cost of getting the children to the school they wanted to go to.

It seemed a simple solution to propose that Government could help by providing free travel for any child who could not walk to school. For able-bodied children, it was decided that if you lived more than two miles from that school, then bus travel would be free.

But, it's like organising a war. Lots of things can go wrong.

One writer complained that the new rules only applied if you went to the nearest High School. But her children had been going to one further away. This meant that **she did not have the right to pick her own school for her children**.

She went on to say that the nearest school did not teach Latin. Did she also **lose her right to choose whatever subjects she wanted**?

Another mother wrote that there was a safe way to walk to school, and also a dangerous way. The dangerous way was just under 2 miles. The Authorities were forcing the children to walk this way. But the mother wanted them to travel on a bus the safe way. This would have been free, because it was just over two miles. Was this fair and sensible, she asked.

A third mother had a slightly impaired child, and lived over a mile from her school. She could "hobble" there on fine days, but when it rained it was too much for her. Could she be given a pass to allow her free bus travel on wet days?

Comment. Pity the poor policy-draftsmen. They were expected to foresee all such situations and get them into legislation in a few weeks. No wonder there were loopholes.

Again, all they could do was fix them. But, of course, the real complaint against so many Government Departments was that they did not fix them in a timely manner.

FEDERAL ELECTION

The election was held on October 25th. We did not end up with a Labor Government. But it was closer than it had been previously.

The Liberals had held a majority of 41 seats. Now they had a lead of only seven. For Labour, Gough Whitlam was on the scene as Leader, and he was getting back die-hard voters who would not vote for the Old Guard of Labor.

Comment. All 125 Seats were won by the two **major parties**. There were **no independents or minor parties**. Contrast this with more recent elections.

NOVEMBER NEWS ITEMS

Every year, a few Unions go on strike not long before Christmas. They, of course, want more money and better working conditions. Sometimes they win, sometimes they lose. Airline pilots can be guaranteed to strike, as can brewery and transport workers....

This year **a new variation** has occurred. Just before **the Melbourne Cup**, the Victorian Trades Hall Council said that their unionists expected to strike on Cup Day. That would have stopped the grand event. They wanted more pay for anyone connected....

The good news is that the day before the race, the strike was cancelled pending talks. **This always happens....**

Bank workers' **Unions** this year decided to get in on the act. They called a strike for Monday, the day before the Cup. That would cause mayhem as punters and bookies sought **money from banks for gambling purposes**....

But the Unions were frustrated. Most bank workers **turned out for work** and ignored the call to strike. As one worker said "It is an opportunistic strike just before the Cup. It won't change anything, and **millions of Australians will have the day spoilt for them**."

The *Sunday Herald* carried a top story to the effect that the Cup **is a two-horse race**. Its so-called experts are tipping that either *Tails* or *Big Philou* will win. The betting market thinks the same, with **the nearest rival a massive 8-1 and all others over 10-1....**

But neither horse won. *Rain Lover* **won by a head** to be **the first horse in 107 years to win successive Cups**.

US President Nixon gave a typically tough speech. He said that the **US will continue** to have forces in Vietnam, despite **the current death toll of 40,000 men**....

His support rating is **still 53 per cent**, showing a steady decline over the year....

Let me get ahead of myself, and say that later this month **there will be events in Vietnam** that will shatter any complacency generated by this majority. They took their toll on support for **the war in Australia** too.

NSW, and other States, will introduce legislation **to provide free legal aid to battlers**. It will be restricted to those who **do not have much income or assets**, and it will be available for certain courts, especially matrimonial courts....

These provisions have widened over the years, and despite seasonal variations, now affect large numbers of proceedings in many different Courts in 2019.

A *SMH* **headline said "Hopes for peace in Middle East dwindle**." I suggest that no person at all read this article. This was not news. It was just headlines that occurred **twice a month**. Either high hopes, or dwindled hopes....

Israel, Palestine, Egypt, and a few other nations were locked into **bitter disputes** that **escalated** 20 years ago in 1949, and **have gone on and on**, with only **a few wars to show for it**, to this present day in 2019.

THE COMMON MARKET

Britain has been talking about joining in with most of the nations of Europe to form a Common Market. The idea here is that about 20 nations will stop placing tariffs on each others' goods, and gradually let all goods move about without any import charges.

Hopes are that this type of Union will bring some political unity, and even mutual defence arrangements.

Fifteen years ago, when talk of such a Market first emerged, there was much concern among businessmen and politicians. Such deals would mean that **our** preferential deals with Britain for agricultural products would be done away with. That would mean that Britain would be free to buy her wheat, say, from anywhere in the world, rather than only from British Empire countries, like Australia.

It had big repercussions for our trading. But as the Brits moved slowly, by 1969 this nation had accepted the inevitability of the Market, and had shifted our trading patterns. For example, by then **we** traded more heavily with China and Japan than with Britain.

So, with the Common Market deal hopefully about to be signed, there was here a lot of curiosity about how it would work, but no great fear. It would still have an effect, but nothing like that of 15 years earlier.

Comment. In 2019, it seems that the UK is on the verge of leaving the Common Market that it so slowly joined half a century ago. At the moment of writing, it is still official UK policy to leave, to BREXIT, but no one would be certain.

If it does go, or even if it does not, scarcely a ripple should be caused here.

DISILLUSIONED ABORIGINES

In the 1960's, the status of Aborigines in society had improved a lot. Governments, both Federal and State, had relaxed rules and restrictions so that they were getting a somewhat fairer deal than before. For example, they were now counted in our national Census, and could now vote. Some of them were allowed to drink alcohol, their housing and education had often improved.

But importantly, the man and woman in the street had changed their attitudes towards Aborigines. Twenty years ago, the average white person could scarcely find a good word for them. Today, in 1969, most white persons know that the Aborigines are getting a rough deal, and would genuinely like to do something to help. What that something was, however, remained a mystery to us all.

This Letter below shows one situation where some efforts were being made, but to what avail?

Letters, Stan Davey, Field research Officer, Aborigines' Advancement League. The Australian Presbyterian Board of Missions, in proposing to hand over responsibility for reserve land near Derby to the Aboriginal residents, is putting into practice the enlightened proposals of the Division of Missions of the Australian Council of Churches.

However, since this land is evidently the Mowanjum Mission, the board would have acted more creditably if it had striven to enable the people to take over a similar area of land in their own tribal area.

Besides the fact that Mowanjum is not the tribal country of the people involved, it is known to be a poor area for a successful company enterprise. Of the 153,000 acres of Mowanjum, one-third is submerged under king tides twice a year; a similar area is dense Pindan country which is costly to clear and impossible to muster cattle in; and an expert cattleman could not raise the land's cattle-carrying capacity to more than 1,500 head. The mission's water supply is one of the worst in the Kimberleys, being too salty to grow even tomatoes.

Mowanjum has become a place of disillusionment and broken promises. When they moved from an earlier mission site, the people believed Native Welfare promised new homes and plenty of good land to move around in, as well as the benefits of education and employment in European society.

Ten years later, most families still live in small, barn-like transitional sheds and share community bathrooms, laundries and toilets. Native Welfare offers them some new houses in Derby, but seems adamant in resisting the building of decent houses in their own village.

The demoralisation of Aboriginal young men and women, and the breaking down of the respect and authority of the elders among their children through the impact of a totally alien educational system, has begun to break the spirit of a proud people.

A move such as that proposed by the Presbyterian Board of Missions could help to restore the fibre and self-respect of this community - but not at Mowanjum. The physical disadvantages are so great it is unrealistic to offer such apparent opportunities on which more highly skilled and sophisticated people could not capitalise.

Comment. What could be done better? Not just on paper but someone needs to find a plan, finance and organise it, and make it happen. Where does anyone start?

There are hundreds, nay, thousands of similar but different situations that also need fixing. **And what a stupid word is that "fixing."** It shows where I am on the matter. I do not even know a word to describe what I want to do. I know I want to improve things, but what, and how, I would do, I have no clue of.

Sad comment from 2019. Nor, I suspect, does anyone else. Over the last 50 years, schemes from well-meaning Governments and other well-wishers, have come and gone. Again, they have gradually improved quite a few things. But overall, the problems remain, and no one, Aboriginal or white, seems any closer to **fixing** them.

POST-ELECTION ELECTION

The Liberals had been accepted back into power by the voters. But it has not been decided who should then lead the Party. There were three contenders.

John Gorton was leader before the election. He was relaxed with a she'll-be-right attitude, who would not be expected to rock the boat. No new policy initiatives could be expected from him.

William McMahon was an ambitious politician who was still Treasurer. He was from Sydney's wealthy Eastern Suburbs and his personality did not register with most of Australia.

David Fairbairn was a surprise nomination who, after the national election, criticised Gorton because he was weak on policy initiatives, and for not doing much.

I enclose just a few of the many Letters on the subject.

Letters, Geoffrey Wood. The "Fairbairn bombshell" could well prove to have the effect of a Molotov cocktail on the structure of the Liberal Party, and hundreds of thousands of Liberal voters, like myself, are grateful that a halt has at last been called to the sickening march of "Gortonism."

For better or worse, the Parliamentary Liberal Party must now choose between getting back to the principles on which the party was founded or continuing its cronyism, centralism, intransigence and arrogance so overwhelmingly rejected by the Australian people.

The choice is now between loyalty on the one hand to the remaining electors who support the Liberal Party and those who would return their support if recent mistakes were recognised, and on the other hand to a so-called leader who is so obtuse or ignorant as to be unable to learn a lesson.

Mr Fairbairn's courageous initiative makes it impossible to hide the distasteful happenings since

Mr Holt's death, or to rationalise them by "closing ranks" behind an increasingly discredited Prime Minister. It is to be hoped that those concerned will rise above petty self-seeking and seize the opportunity to restore liberalism, vitality and unity to the Liberal Party.

Letters, Malcolm Hardwick. The person who would be forming the new Government would not be Mr Gorton (the people's choice), but either Mr McMahon or Mr David Fairbairn, to be chosen behind closed doors at a secret ballot of 65 or 66 people in defiance of the people's will.

It is impossible to believe that the Federal Parliamentary Liberal Party is so singularly lacking in what ought to be the most elementary political sense as not to realise that were its members now to reject Mr Gorton in the face of and so soon after the mandate given him by the Australian people to form another government, then, more likely than not, they would ensure for many years to come a sustained and continued rejection by the Australian people of themselves and the Liberal Party at least at Canberra or even elsewhere.

Letters, John Stokie. Mr Gorton is lucky he is only a leader of a political party and not a leader of an army, when at the first setback some of his lieutenants rat on him.

Both they and some of the public seem to have forgotten that only a small section of the electors swing the vote and on this occasion thousands of fond mothers voted against the Government on account of the Vietnam issue, which added impetus to the swing.

No doubt Mr Gorton would like to pull out of Vietnam, but he realises our dependence on America for some years to come. He has to think of Australia first; and, to boil it down, Mr Gorton was not Prime Minister when National Service was introduced.

There is an old saying that rats desert a sinking ship, but I hope there will be enough courageous men in the Liberal Party to stand strongly behind their leader to maintain the prosperity the country is enjoying.

I looked for active supporters of McMahon, but could find none.

Comment. The truth was that no one of them appeared to have the support of a majority of the Party. **Whoever won was likely to be undermined by the losers and their supporters.**

Whitlam was the fly in the ointment for all three. He was on a roll. He had just gained many seats in the national elections, and his policies, and speeches, and changes to the Old Guard were sweeping all before him. All three Liberal candidates seemed poor by comparison. Whoever from among them won the Leadership was seen to be just keeping the Prime Minister's seat warm until Labor could mount another challenge.

GLOVES OFF OVER KINDERS

The kindergarten debate had been quiet for a few months, but it heated up again. A few suggestions had been made that the provision of kinders was not only good for the national economy, but it was vital to mobilising the female labour force and thereby maximising our national output.

Most women, however, now saw kinders as a possible means of increasing family income, and perhaps as a good way to give the children valuable personal skills.

In any case, mothers were up in arms, though there was strong dissent among their ranks.

Letters, (Mrs) Joan Vivian. As one of many parents who did not or do not send their children to pre-school kindergarten - preferring them to reap the richer benefits of early life in and around that "nursery of the infinite," the home, be it ever so humble - I feel so sorry for the mother who, through necessity, selfishness or ignorance, sends her child away to an establishment at the tender years of three to five.

Not only does she miss many joys and responsibilities of motherhood which should be a continuous, maturing growth, but her child is deprived of many natural and simple pleasures and learning as unfolded to him and as he sees and discovers through his own senses.

There is another kind of mother who deserves not only pity but rescue: the one who sends her child to pre-school kindergarten because her preserves of maternal instincts and know-how have been so heavily trespassed upon by the advice of child experts on how to be a mother, that she has become like the centipede who "was happy quite until a toad, in fun, said: 'Pray, which leg comes after which?'"

Letters, (Mrs) Margaret Turpin. As one of the many mothers who through "necessity, selfishness and ignorance" chooses to send her children to preschool kindergarten, perhaps I should hang my head in shame at the discovery of my own base motives, hitherto undetected.

Our children attend kindergarten for six hours a day, during which time, apart from enjoying the company of others their own age, they learn to acquire basic skills with equipment and material especially provided for them. They also learn that they have to give and take with their fellows, and manage to reach a degree of independence that stands them in good stead when they are suddenly propelled into school at the age of five.

While it would be hypocritical to deny that there are some mornings when we breathe a sigh of relief when our little darlings are safely off to "an establishment" (shades of Dickens), so that we may indulge in such selfish activities as a game of golf, shopping in peace, or a visit to the hairdresser, we are equally delighted to be reunited with them a few hours later, especially when an excited infant, brandishing a futuristic painting, nearly bowls us over to shout, "Look what I did at kinder today, mummy!"

Weekends and holidays give our children ample time to indulge in "the natural and simple pleasures" mentioned by Mrs Joan Vivian. In my son's case, these range from getting stuck in the washing machine to cutting his sister's hair and bunging ex-friend's pantie hose up the exhaust of ex-friend's car.

Yes, we certainly miss a lot by sending our children to preschool kindergarten, but let's have more of them so that other unfortunate mothers, full of selfishness and ignorance, may share my guilt complex.

Comment. As you can see, these arguments were getting a bit touchy. But the above Letters reflect different ways of doing the job of being a good mother. It was not the case of who was good and who was bad. It was just that some saw their children as being best served by kinder years, and others saw them better served at home.

Since then, perhaps because many of them experienced kinders as children themselves, many more children are going off to kinder. **And of course, the Federal Government is subsiding this.**

Second comment. While ever the nation can afford it, I think there is nothing wrong with this. The littlies I know enjoy it a lot, and are no more repulsive than the home brood.

THE MY LAI MASSACRE

November 17th.   News Item. A group of Vietnamese villagers was awakened by an hour of shell-fire on the morning of March 16th, 1968. Then a small unit of American soldiers walked into the village without opposition. The villages were ordered into three groups, about 200 yards apart. Their houses were burned.

The inhabitants were gunned down where they stood. 567 men, women and children were killed. The executions were carried out by about 20 soldiers at each site, using their individual weapons, presumably standard issue MK-16 rifles.

The Lieutenant in charge, William Halley, has been held and it is suggested that he might face Court Marshall. Other soldiers might face charges as well.

Comment. This My Lai massacre was reported **now** only because it had been covered up for 18 months by all concerned.

November 28th. Press report. After an initial investigation, President Nixon admitted that the offence as described had occurred. He expressed his horror at the act, and said that the nation found it abhorrent.

More details he said, will be released after further investigation.

Second comment. The world was **horrified**. Everyone was accustomed to the US reporting war atrocities by the enemy. Now to find out that the American forces were just as guilty was a great shock.

The US, too, was horrified. Even the fiercest supporter of the war was mortified, and the anti-war groups stepped up their opposition.

But that was not the end of this story. I will come back to it next month.

WHO WILL BE PRIME MINISTER?

John Gorton, of course. He won the position with a Parliamentary Party vote of 53 per cent. This was on the first and only ballot, so his victory should be seen as a convincing one. He should have little trouble controlling dissident factions within the Party - for a while.

Unsuccessful candidate Bill McMahon was moved from Treasury to Foreign Affairs. He was still in a position where he could breathe down the Prime Minister's neck.

David Fairbairn, who had been too violent in his criticism of Gorton, was "relieved of his Cabinet responsibilities".

SUNDAY DRINKING

The Referendum to decide NSW's Sunday drinking regime was held on November 29th. It was a victory for the NO vote.

That is, 60 per cent of the citizen voted **against** opening local pubs on Sundays. In terms of electorates, 88 voted against opening, and only six voted for it.

Generally, opinion was that voters thought that the death and injury toll on the road would be increased by the opening. Another reason given was that families wanted a day at home to catch their breath. A third group said that there was ample time available for drinking already.

So, if you want a drink on Sunday, just wait a while. The issue will be back soon enough.

DECEMBER NEWS ITEMS

The NSW country city of Parkes has an associate Branch of the Australian **Hotels Association** there. This branch has **voted to ban Salvation Army collections in its bars** because last week the collection officer handed out how-to-vote cards in bars. **The cards advocated voting NO.**

The **Federal Minister for Shipping and Transport** was scheduled to open some function in Perth but his car did not arrive. He was forced to hitch-hike. He was picked up by **a housewife in curlers, with her three children** on the way to school. **How very Australian.**

A Boeing 707 aircraft, carrying 136 passengers, **ploughed into a cloud of seagulls** just before take-off at Sydney's Mascot airport. It braked, and skidded to a halt in deep mud at the end of the run-way....

No one was hurt, everyone was muddy and shaken, and many passengers spent the next two hours **drinking their duty-free Scotch in the airport lounge.**

Four miners found **a crystal opal** at Andamuka last month. It weighed about **17 Pound**s, or eight Kilograms. It sold yesterday for **$168,000. It is the largest opal ever found in Australia.**

The Sydney Branch Of the Waterside Workers Federation has **decided not to load military supplies due to be sent to our troops in Vietnam** on the supply ship **Jeparit**....

The Branch says it opposes the war, and after the My Lai massacre, would do nothing to keep it going....

Opinion in Australia is strongly opposed to the Branch. Regardless of their opinions on the war, they are conscious that Australian lives will be lost if supplies of arms and munitions are not delivered to Vietnam. They say that the ship should be loaded.

December 5th. Poseidon shares reached $65.

South Australia will be the first Australian State to legalise abortion. Approval must be given by two doctors, and there is a prior residency period of four months living in the State. Abortions can only be performed at a prescribed hospital....

The other States are still struggling with the issue, and might take a long time to make up their minds.

Seven bathers **will be prosecuted for appearing nude on a remote part of the beach in Bondi**, Sydney. These are the first such prosecutions since 1926.

A young boy aged 12 had three stitches inserted in his face after being hit by a toy boomerang.

December 9th. Poseidon shares climbed to $75.

The last News item of the year. Twenty students barricaded themselves inside a South Australian University building as a protest, as John Gorton visited the building. Nothing special here, but an appropriate way **to end a year that was dominated by Vietnam**.

Final message of the year. **Christmas is here again. But don't despair.** It only lasts a few weeks and then life can go on again.

HIT SONGS OF 1969

Ob-La-Di, Ob-La-Da	The Beatles
Honky Tonk Women	Rolling Stones
Something	The Beatles
Where Do You Go To (My Lovely)	Peter Sarstedt
In the Ghetto	Elvis Presley
Get Back	The Beatles
The Girl That I Love	Russell Morris
Hair	The Cowsills
The Real Thing	Russell Morris
Penny Arcade	Roy Orbison
Eloise	Barry Ryan

TOP MOVIES OF 1969

Butch Cassidy and the Sundance Kid
        Robert Redford, Paul Newman

Midnight Cowboy
        Dustin Hoffman, Jon Voight

On Her Majesty's Secret Service
        George Lazenby, Diana Rigg

Easy Rider   **Peter Fonda, Dennis Hopper**

The Italian Job   **Michael Caine, Noel Coward**

The Wild Bunch   **William Holden, Robert Ryan**

True Grit   **John Wayne, Glen Campbell**

Goodbye, Columbus Richard Benjamin, Ali McGraw

Paint Your Wagon   Lee Marvin, Clint Eastwood

Hello Dolly!   **Barbra Streisand, Walter Matthau**

Age of Consent   James Mason, Helen Mirren

JAZZ

Complaints keep coming in about the demise of Jazz music on the ABC. And about the composition of the jazz programmes that do exist. Listeners remember back in 1949 when Dixieland jazz was commonly played, when *Mississippi Mud* was hummed by everyone, when Rag Time was all the go. *Listen to that tenor saxophone, never heard it played in such a tone. And what about the licorice stick....*

Now the jazz that is played is mellow, perfectly formulated, full of syrup. And the world is filled with electric guitars and other noise makers.

Comment. That is how I felt in 1969. Imagine what I feel now.

GETTING SIGNED - IN

Letters, Derek Freeman. I suggest that Election Form 40 relating to postal voting in Federal elections by Australians overseas, be amended forthwith. The number of Australians travelling overseas at any one time runs into many thousands, but the conditions necessary to make their postal votes valid obviously were drawn up when the "Queen's Dominions" covered a far greater area of the world.

After applying for and receiving a ballot paper for the recent Federal elections while in Florida, I discovered that my vote had to be witnessed by:

(1) An elector who is on the roll in Australia.

(2) A military officer of the Commonwealth or some

other part of the Queen's Dominions.

(3) A Public servant of the above.

(4) A JP, minister of religion or medical practitioner resident in the Commonwealth or a part of the Queen's Dominions.

A diligent search to fulfil such anachronistic conditions proved fruitless, and I object to being disenfranchised in this manner.

Comment. Meandering. This was, and is still, a legitimate complaint. In some cases, a JP could do the job. But in many others, the trustworthy official is impossible to find. In 1969, I had a document witnessed by a Public Servant. He was a junior 16-year-old porter at Abermain Railway Station, but he could aver that I was who I was.

At the time at least, it was all a big joke. Everyone knew that no one would follow up, or check signatures. Yet having said that, once in London, I was at Australia House. I needed an Australian Public Servant to verify something, and gave the details of an old mate, then living retired in the country city of Kempsey.

Half an hour later, when I got to my digs, I rang him to say he might get a call from London. He told me that that had happened 25 minutes ago. So, sometimes, checks were done.

IS POT COMING

A small number of people are talking about legalising pot. They argue that it does no more harm the alcohol, and that it carries no ill effects. That for the young, it is more readily available than alcohol, and that to legalise it would save youth from having to mix with criminals.

Letters, Joseph Alsop, Los Angeles. We are reaching a stage that is unhappily reminiscent of the last years of prohibition, when I was an undergraduate at Harvard. At that time, alcohol's illegality made it immensely and most harmfully fashionable among the young. In the same fashion, illegality has now made pot immensely fashionable - although the fashion has yet to reach its predictable peak.

Among my contemporaries who became alcoholics, I would guess that two of every three suffered this tragic fate because getting falling-down drunk was the fashionable thing to do when they were young and foolish. Fortunately, however, the percentage of real potheads among fairly regular pot smokers appears to be substantially lower than the percentage of real alcoholics among social drinkers.

Comment. This writer says that it seemed certain that pot will be legalised very soon. As it turned out, that has not happened.

I leave it to the reader to work out who has opposed it for 50 years. Do you think their combined force will **ever** be overcome?

Second comment. Take a moment to wonder at how simple we all were in 1969. We were worried then about **pot.** We had no idea of the horrors that **the drugs of the future** would bring.

NEW REFERENDUM QUESTION

Letters, Tired Family Man. It seems unfortunate that in Saturday's referendum we were not also asked to vote on the following day-of-rest "trading" problem.

"Are you in favour of certain Churches continuing their age-long practice of clanging their bells about 60 times at 7 a.m. (or earlier) on Sundays, and another 45 times at 7.25 a.m., the latter to ensure that, if you are not completely woken the first time, the second time will be a certainty."

Comment. This Letter reminds us that most cities and large towns had churches that rang their bells on Sunday mornings, as a summons to the faithful. Also, most Catholic Churches rang their bells every day at 6am, noon, and 6pm to remind their congregations to recite the Angelus.

Some people loved these bells, and many hated them. Some of them had very skilled people who came in and gave grand performances of bell-ringing. However, as the world about us paid less attention to religion, and as church attendance tumbled, the arguments for keeping the tolling became less convincing. So much so, that many of the belfries round the nation have seen their bells removed.

Second Comment. Old people, when they get together, sometimes get the party going by falling back on the now-forgotten custom of telling jokes. Corny old jokes, that are sexist, racist, and uncharitable, but they are clever and really funny, and make oldies laugh.

My stock in trade for years has been to tell two bell-ringer jokes. They are a bit shaggy-dog, and the first one ends with the punch line "His face rings a bell." The second ends with "He's a dead ringer for his brother."

You can see my difficulty. Now that the bell ringers have gone from our lives, and many of the oldies have died, whenever I tell these jokes, more and more blank faces show up among the young. "What is the silly old bugger talking about?"

And, indeed, I wonder at the moment, **what am I talking about**. Rambling on, I am, about jokes and bells, and this idea of laughing. **It's all so old world.**

I will excuse myself, as I pull myself together, by saying that at the end of each book, I sometimes go a bit mad. Just for a few pages, and then I behave myself.

And that is what I will do. Now. Back to my previous sober self. No frivolous meanderings.

MY LAI LETTERS

Letter writers were predictable as the drama of My Lai unfolded. Those who opposed the war were vehement in their response, those who supported it showed as yet no sign of wavering. That will come later.

The *SMH* issued a wishy-washy Editorial. It pointed out that excesses are to be expected in all wars, and that the North Vietnamese soldiers had done **worse** things. It went on to say that the American authorities were doing all things right in investigating and then possibly bringing charges. "There is every reason to believe that the truth will be published and the guilty punished. Nothing else will satisfy the American sense of justice."

This was a bit limp under the circumstances. Whatever political game the *SMH* was playing, it left many people disappointed.

One such person also had a distinctive stance.

> **Letters, Ian Farr**. I found the attitude of your editorial on My Lai totally depressing. So war is a kind of game and should be played strictly according to the rules; that way we can wage war with a clear conscience. Is this what civilisation has done for us?
>
> So long as there are wars there will be My Lais, and so long as the powerful influencers of public opinion such as "The Sydney Morning Herald" condone these wars, **no amount of sophistry** of this kind will be able to excuse them for encouraging men to degrade themselves so that they are unfit to live together on this earth.
>
> I, for one, don't wish to stay around long enough to live through too many more My Lais, Hues, Sharpvilles, Hiroshimas, Lidices, or whatever new horrors such concepts of civilisation and enlightenment lead us into.

VIETNAM AFTER MY LAI

Slowly, America accepted the fact that the My Lai massacre had actually happened. Images from the scene came to light, soldiers present at the time admitted it. But in addition, when the walls of a dam is breached, so the whole dam collapses.

So, in the months after My Lai - and now I am leaking next year's story - **more accusations were brought forward** about other, equally horrible, events with a similar theme. That was, that US soldiers had bombed, strafed, and killed many, many Vietnamese villagers for no good reason. At times, it seemed like a sport, it was so capricious.

On top of this, reports emerged, and were subsequently verified, that the US Air Force was dropping bombs onto forest to clear the foliage. But the villagers were taking shelter from attack in the forests, and so they were being burned to death. This atrocity was found to be widespread.

Over the course of the next year or so, as these stories were revealed to the US public, opposition to the war increased at the same pace as the outrage. From these days forward, it was clear that the Americans would have to find a way out of the Vietnam war.

SUMMING UP 1969

First let me assure you that **economically** our nation was humming along pretty well. Tons of jobs, a reasonable security blanket for the unfortunates, housing getting better, Aborigines were on the improve, politicians the same as ever, sport at the weekend, and fewer and fewer church-goers on Sundays. A mixed bag, one that left most people reasonably happy.

This was not true of course for those people who wanted the Vietnam war to end. There was a growing number of these, and it was possible to see that the war would not go on forever. But for these, it was a painful period, with no rest for the families close to the action. Or, let us not forget, **for the soldiers in the front line either**.

Apart from that, the world was not destroyed by atom bombs, and they were not used to build harbours. On the darker side, housie-housie was a menace to society, though it **was** threatened here by the bountiful clubs. Asians were coming here for good, their nurses were swelling the list of unhappy people in hospitals, and the Brits were buying only a little bit of our wheat.

People were walking on the moon, and there was a potential for litter to become a problem there, and on our streets. Meanwhile, the Bong Bong picnic races went on, and our Aborigines edged towards a better life. Conditions in remand were bad, but you had a chance that a kind magistrate would show you mercy.

But in all, Australia was a good place to be, and to grow up in. I can find no better place anywhere, and I might add, no better time to be born. After a few more years of war, not invasion, there was at least 50 years ahead without any really upsetting events, lots of prosperity, and a social cohesion that is the envy of the world.

I hope you will not think me frivolous when I end with the rallying call of :

LONG LIVE 1969

In 1950, Dugan and Mears used a hacksaw to break out of gaol, robbed banks, shot people and went back to gaol. The War finished five years ago, so it was time to stop petrol rationing. War criminals were hanging out at Nuremberg. Dancing pumps were tripping the light fantastic at The Plaza. Whaling in Australia was big; square dancing was bigger.

In 1951, the coal miners' funds were declared black. The great mower war disturbed Sunday's peace. General MacArthur was given the boot. Hire purchase was buying vacuum cleaners. Sunday films and sport were driving clergy frantic. Farmers were hopping mad over a kangaroo glut.

****

Chrissi and birthday books for Mum and Dad and Aunt and Uncle and cousins and family and friends and work and everyone else.

Don't forget a good read and chuckle for yourself.

In 1952, Bob (Menzies) was not your uncle. Women smokers were keeping the home fires burning. Sid Barnes jumped a turnstile and suited himself. US and China were still happily killing each other, and millions of Koreans were collateral damage. Some horses were entering a grey area. Women voted to do jury duty at their convenience.

****

These 35 soft cover books are available from all good book store and newsagents.